Canadian Concepts 4

Lynda Berish
Sandra Thibaudeau

Prentice Hall Canada Inc., Scarborough, Ontario

Canadian Cataloguing in Publication Data

Berish, Lynda, 1952–
Canadian concepts 4

ISBN 0-13-096918-4

1. English language – Textbooks for second
language learners.* 2. English language – Grammar –
1950– . 3. English language – Grammar –
Problems, exercises, etc.   I. Thibaudeau,
Sandra, 1943– .   II. Title.

PE1128.B37 1993   428.2'4   C92-094778-6

Prentice-Hall, Inc., Englewood Cliffs, New Jersey
Prentice-Hall International, Inc., London
Prentice-Hall of Australia, Pty., Ltd., Sydney
Prentice-Hall of India Pvt., Ltd., New Delhi
Prentice-Hall of Japan, Inc., Tokyo
Prentice-Hall of Southeast Asia (Pte.) Ltd., Singapore
Editora Prentice-Hall do Brasil Ltda., Rio de Janeiro
Prentice-Hall Hispanoamericana, S.A., Mexico

ISBN 0-13-096918-4

Acquisitions editor: Marjorie Walker
Developmental editor: Linda Gorman
Production editor: Elynor Kagan
Production coordinator: Lisa Kreuch/Anita Boyle
Design and layout: Joseph Chin
Illustrations: Paul McCusker
Audio cassettes: Morris Apelbaum, Silent Sound Studio, Montreal
Cover design: Aurora Di Ciaula
Cover illustration: June Bradford

1 2 3 4 5   97 96 95 94 93

Printed and bound in Canada by Webcom Limited

Contents

To the Teacher

The *Canadian Concepts* Series

The *Canadian Concepts* Series is a six-book series designed for students learning English in Canada. Survival topics and cultural information based on Canadian themes help students integrate into the community. These themes are recycled with increasing complexity throughout the series. Practical topics in the lower levels progress to topics of interest and concern to more advanced students.

The *Canadian Concepts* Series is communicative in approach. The method offers productive strategies for language learning based on student-centred interaction. The pedagogical model presents students with challenging input, and provides activities that involve the students in information exchange. Students are often asked to work in pairs or groups to extend their understanding through interaction. Fluency activities are supported with spelling, dictation, pronunciation and writing tasks that focus on accuracy.

Canadian Concepts 4

Students using *Canadian Concepts 4* are challenged by rich and complex input that introduces a variety of interesting themes. Students are asked to participate in activities that call on them to use natural language and to explain and express opinions.

Teachers and students will appreciate the simplicity of the materials. Clear illustrations provide visual support and stimulate student discussion. Worksheets for some activities are provided in a special section of the Teacher's Manual, with permission to photocopy.

The Units

Canadian Concepts 4 is divided into 12 self-contained units. The units focus on themes that are interesting and relevant to the students.

Each unit begins with an overview of topics and activities. The unit is then made up of a variety of activities that follow a basic three-part pattern. The first section introduces the subject. The next section calls for students to work with challenging material in the core reading or listening activity. Then the language is reviewed in a variety of ways.

The Activities

The "Get Ready" section provides reading or listening preparation. These pre-activities introduce the topic and generate interest in a variety of ways: through prediction exercises, discussion questions, dictation or interaction. The Teacher's Manual provides suggestions for warm-up activities to do before students open their books.

Core activities focus on taped passages, reading texts and video materials. They promote strategies of guessing from context, trying out possible answers and revising understanding through successive steps. Core activities consist of a variety of tasks: reading or listening for general information, reading or listening for detailed information, and drawing information from video programmes.

Follow-up activities recycle language in the unit, providing an opportunity for students to express themselves and use new vocabulary. They include discussion activities, opportunities to practise language, vocabulary review, grammar review and writing.

Pre-Activities	Core Activities	Review and Recycle	Real-Life Application
Get Ready to Read	Read for General Ideas	Review Vocabulary	Role Play
Get Ready to Listen	Read for Details	Review Expressions	Exchange Information
Get Ready to Discuss	Read to Increase Speed	Practise Speaking	What About You?
Get Ready to Watch the Video	Listen for Meaning	Practise Grammar	Express Yourself
	Listen for Details	Practise Writing	Community Contact Tasks
	Watch the Video for General Ideas	Practise Numbers	
	Watch the Video for Details	Transfer Information	
		Use Information	
		Dictation	
		Tell the Story	
		Write the Story	

Key to Symbols

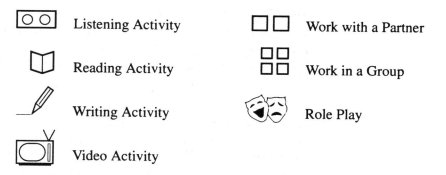

Listening Activity	Work with a Partner
Reading Activity	Work in a Group
Writing Activity	Role Play
Video Activity	

Listening Programme

The listening programme in *Canadian Concepts 4* consists of dialogues and short listening passages and video activities. Students listen to natural-sounding Canadian English on topics of interest. They are able to move through stages of comprehension as they listen first for general meaning and then for details. Finally, they use the information in a variety of ways.

Passages are recorded two or three times in sequence so that teachers will not have to hunt for material on the tape during the class. Complete listening scripts are provided in the Teacher's Manual.

Video Programme

The video programme is an exciting new element beginning in Level 4. High quality *National Geographic* educational videos provide opportunities for students to listen for information delivered in natural English. Pre-activities prepare the students to meet the challenge of richer, longer input. Follow-up activities allow them to reuse and consolidate new vocabulary and structures. The videos used in *Canadian Concepts 4* are:

Farming
The Four Seasons: Spring
Families Around the World: Mexico

These videos can be purchased directly from the National Geographic Society, Educational Services, 211 Watline Avenue, Mississauga, Ontario L4Z 1P3 (Telephone 416-890-1111).

Supplementary Grammar

Explanations of grammar points and practice exercises are provided in the Supplementary Grammar section. These exercises also review vocabulary from the preceding units. Suggestions for introducing grammar points are given in the Teacher's Manual.

Community Contact Tasks

The Community Contact Tasks are designed to complement activities done in class. They are linked to units in the book. Students have an opportunity to practise their English in real-life situations outside the classroom. A variety of tasks has been provided so that a selection can be made according to the needs and interests of the students in a particular class. Worksheets are provided in the Teacher's Manual.

Teacher's Manual

Each book in the series has its own Teacher's Manual that includes:

- step-by-step instructions keyed to the student's book;

- suggestions for classroom interaction;

- answers for exercises;

- tape scripts for listening activities;

- teacher's scripts for dictations and pronunciation exercises;

- student worksheets.

Detailed teacher's notes are included to make the intention of activities clear and to guide new teachers. Experienced teachers will find that the material lends itself to flexibility and accommodates individual teaching styles.

The authors wish success to their colleagues and the students who use these Canadian materials.

Acknowledgements

We would like to acknowledge the support and assistance of the following people in the classroom testing of the materials in this book: Maria De Rosa Wilson, Pat Singh, Linda Moore and Geoff Blake. Their valuable comments, support and suggestions have been much appreciated.

We would like to thank several people who have offered particular encouragement to the *Canadian Concepts* project: Jerry Smith, Marjorie Walker, Kedre Murray, Linda Gorman and Yolanda de Rooy. We would also like to express thanks for the technical expertise provided by Morris Apelbaum, Gail Ferreira-Ng-A-Kien, Marta Tomins and Joe Chin and for the invaluable editorial assistance of Elynor Kagan.

Our thanks go also to our families for the patience and help they have extended: to our husbands, John Berish and Charles Gruss, and our children, Tara and Andrea Berish and Jean-Baptiste, Gabrielle and Annabel Thibaudeau. We would also like to express appreciation to Zorana Prelevic and C.E. Eckersley for inspiration and encouragement, and to Max and Millicent Goldman who, over many years and in many ways, have offered the kind of encouragement writers need to keep going.

The World

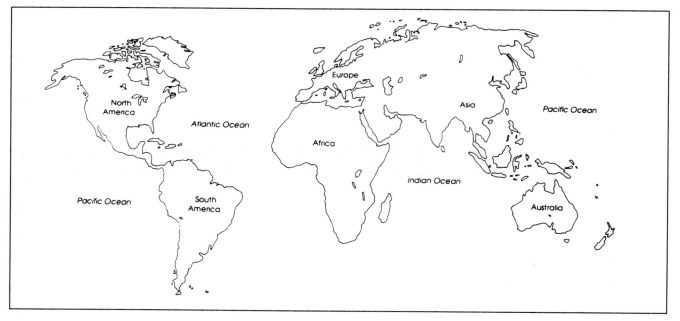

Canada

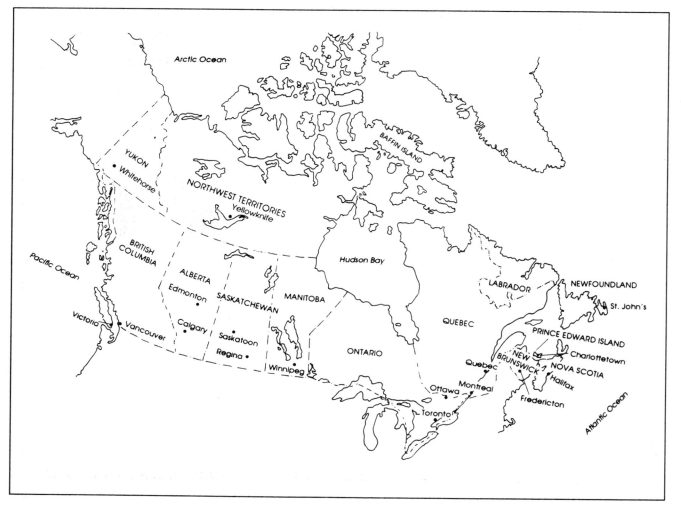

Unit 1

Meeting People

Greetings
Discussion
Reading
Cultural Information

Grammar Point
Each Other

What About You?
Information Exchange
Writing

Small Talk
Listening Activity 1

Meeting a Friend
Role Play

Greetings

Exercise 1: Get Ready to Read

Discuss these questions in a group.

1. What do you say when you meet a person for the first time in your culture?

2. Do you shake hands, or do you use another way of greeting people in your culture?

3. Are there any rules about shaking hands in your culture?

4. What kind of handshake do you prefer? What kind of handshake do you not like?

5. In your culture, is it common to hug or kiss people that you greet?

Exercise 2: Read Quickly for General Ideas

Greetings

Everywhere in the world people follow certain customs when they meet, but in different cultures people follow different customs. In most western countries, the custom when two people meet is to shake hands. So when two people meet for the first time, they usually hold each other's hands briefly, shake once or twice and let go. Two old friends often hold hands a little longer than strangers do. They may even embrace. They may hug each other or kiss each other on the cheek.

NICE TO MEET YOU.

The custom of shaking hands probably began long ago when a stranger was always a possible enemy. Two strangers who met opened their hands to show that they were not armed. Then they took and held each other's hands as a sign of friendship. This custom still exists today as a handshake of greeting.

Among the Inuit in northern Canada, the traditional greeting is to touch noses. Some people think that the reason for this custom is the climate. In very cold weather it is dangerous to remove your gloves to shake hands. Because people's faces aren't covered, it is easier for them to rub noses when they meet.

In eastern countries there are a variety of different customs. In India, for example, the traditional Hindu greeting is made by joining the palms of both hands together and holding them in front of the face. Pictures of Ghandi show him making this gesture of peace and welcome. In Indonesia, people shake hands, but it is usually men who shake hands with men and women who shake hands with women.

Indonesians often say their name as they shake hands with someone they are meeting for the first time. This is a way to introduce themselves.

In Japan people bow. Bowing is a very formal custom in Japanese society. When two people meet, the junior person bows first. When the senior person bows, the junior person bows more deeply to show respect. Some Japanese department stores have greeters who stand at the door and bow to the customers.

Exercise 3: Read Carefully for Details

Work with a partner. Look for the answers in the text.

1. Where is handshaking common?
2. What are the three steps that people follow when they shake hands?
3. What are three signs that people are old friends?
4. Where does the custom of shaking hands come from?
5. What is the traditional greeting among the Inuit?
6. What is the traditional Hindu greeting?
7. Who is often shown using this greeting?
8. Is it common for all Indonesians to shake hands?
9. What do Indonesians say when they meet for the first time?
10. Give two rules the Japanese follow when they bow.

Exercise 4: Review Vocabulary

Match words that mean the opposite.

first	today
friend	hold
stand	longer
always	last
long ago	enemy
let go	sit
western	never
shorter	eastern

Did You Know?   Some Canadians use handshaking as a public greeting. Other Canadians kiss each other on the cheek, or hug quickly to greet each other.

Grammar Point

When people complete an action together, the expression **each other** is used. Look at the examples below.

Romeo and Juliet kissed **each other**.

The students in this class often help **each other**.

Victor and Jill shook hands with **each other**.

What About You?

Exercise 1: Get Ready

 Interview another person in the class. Here are some questions you can ask:

1. Where are you from?

2. What languages do you speak?

3. How do you say "hello" in your language?

4. What are some greeting customs in your culture? (Do you shake hands, hug, etc.)

5. Why do you want to study English?

Exercise 2: Write

Write about the person you interviewed.

Exercise 3: Discuss

Work in a group. Tell the other students in the group about the person you interviewed.

Small Talk

> **Listening Activity 1**

Exercise 1: Get Ready to Listen

 In a group, discuss these subjects.

1. Which subjects do people talk about when they first meet?

2. Which subjects do people not talk about in Canada?

their health	religion	things in the news
the weather	food	salaries
sports	people they know	cars
their jobs	their ages	clothes
their families	their education	politics

 Exercise 2: Listen for General Ideas

1. Where are these people?
2. How many people are talking?
3. Who are the people?
   a) friends
   b) relatives
   c) colleagues

6

Exercise 3: Listen for Details

Cover Exercise 4.

As you listen, answer the questions. Answer true (**T**) or false (**F**).

1. Nick knows Carla from school.
2. Mike and Nick are good friends.
3. Nick works at the Bay.
4. Nick's job is exciting.
5. Carla and Mike met each other at school.
6. Carla is looking for a summer job.
7. The Bay has summer jobs for students.
8. The sporting goods department sells food.
9. Nick is in a hurry and has to go.
10. They decide to sit and talk in a restaurant.

Exercise 4: Practise Speaking

In a group of three, practise the conversation.

Small Talk

Nick:	Hi Mike. How are you doing?
Mike:	Fine thanks. Nice to see you Nick. Have you met Carla?
Nick:	No, I haven't. Nice to meet you, Carla.
Carla:	Hi Nick. Nice to meet you too. Mike has told me a lot about you. Do you still have that job at the Bay?
Nick:	Yes. It's boring but the pay is good. How do you two know each other?
Mike:	Carla and I are old friends. Our parents live on the same street. Carla's a student. She's looking for a summer job.
Carla:	Do you think there are any jobs for students at the Bay?
Nick:	Sure. I'm a student too. I have this job for the summer. I work in the sporting goods department. We sell tennis rackets, footballs, running shoes and all that.
Mike:	Say Nick, are you in a hurry? Let's not stand on the street corner. Do you have time for a coffee?
Carla:	There's a restaurant here. Why don't we have a coffee?
Nick:	Thanks. That's a good idea. Let's sit down in the restaurant while we talk.

Meeting a Friend

Role Play

Work in a group of three. Take different roles.

Imagine that you meet a friend you haven't seen for a long time on the street. You are with another friend.

Write a conversation. Be prepared to perform it for the class.

Here are some expressions to use when you meet:

> Have you met my roommate Nick?
> This is my teacher Richard.
> May I introduce my sister Maria.

Unit 2

Fashion

The Fashion Quiz

Exercise 1: Get Ready

What do you know about fashion? Do this quiz to find out. Work in a group. Discuss the answers to these questions. More than one answer can be correct.

When you have finished, turn to page 18 to check your answers.

1. The first blue jeans were worn by:
   a) miners
   b) teenagers
   c) movie stars

2. The first shoes were:
   a) boots
   b) loafers
   c) sandals

3. Shoes with left feet and right feet were first made in:
   a) 200 BC
   b) 500 AD
   c) 1100 AD

4. The bikini first became popular in Europe, in:
   a) France
   b) Italy
   c) Sweden

5. Men first started wearing long pants:
   a) around 1700
   b) around 1800
   c) around 1920

6. Buttons were first used:
   a) to fasten clothing
   b) to hide things
   c) as decoration

7. A natural fibre that comes from a plant is:
   a) silk
   b) wool
   c) cotton

8. In the 1960s in North America, teenagers wore:
   a) bell-bottom jeans
   b) long hair
   c) leather jackets

9. Gloves were first made from:
   a) linen
   b) animal skins
   c) wool

10. In the 1600s, men wore:
    a) high-heeled shoes
    b) silk stockings
    c) suspenders

11. Men sometimes wear skirts in:
    a) Greece
    b) Scotland
    c) China

12. A man wears a tuxedo to go to:
    a) a wedding
    b) a hockey game
    c) work

Where Do Clothes Come From?

Exercise 1: Get Ready to Read

Work in a group. Look at the pictures.

1. Describe some different clothes that you see people wearing.

2. What are some reasons that people wear different kinds of clothes?

3. How do you think people decide what to wear (which colours to choose, what styles to buy)?

Exercise 2: Read Quickly for General Ideas

Where Do Clothes Come From?

How do we choose the clothes we wear? Often we choose clothes that will protect us from the weather. In cold climates we wear warm clothes made of wool or animal skins. In hot climates we wear light clothes made of cotton. When the weather is very hot, as it is in the Arabian desert, people wear long, loose clothes. These kinds of clothes give protection from the hot sun and let air in to help the people stay cool.

People also choose their clothes for the jobs they do. The police, bus drivers and airplane pilots wear uniforms. Astronauts, divers and miners wear clothes that protect them while they do their work.

In the past, most people made their own clothes. Women used cloth to make clothes for themselves and their families. Later, people sometimes went to a dressmaker or tailor who made clothes for them. Most of the time, rich people copied the styles of kings, queens and people of the courts. When kings or queens wore a new style, people copied it. Travellers got ideas for new styles from other groups of people when they began to visit distant parts of the globe.

Today, high fashion designs from Europe, and more recently from Japan, are sold internationally. Fashion centres such as New York, Montreal and other cities produce their own designs. People no longer copy the styles of kings and queens. Now they want to look like their favourite movie stars and singers.

Many styles today are international. People in many countries in the world wear blue jeans and T-shirts. Leather jackets, saris and kimonos migrate from one culture to another too. When we see new fashions in the stores and in magazines, we want to be in style, so we buy new clothes. People would not buy new clothes so often if the styles did not change so much!

The kind of clothes we wear tell people about us. We wear one kind of clothes to work. We wear a different kind of clothes to relax at home after work or to go to a party. What kind of clothes do you wear?

Exercise 3: Read Carefully for Details

1. What kind of clothes do people need to wear in cold climates?
2. What kind of clothes do people wear in hot climates?
3. Give some examples of people who wear uniforms.
4. Why do astronauts and miners need to wear special clothes?
5. Name two places that people's clothes came from in the past.
6. Where did rich people get their ideas about style?
7. Where do fashion designs come from today?

8. What styles do people copy today?

9. Give some examples of international styles.

10. Why do people like to buy new clothes?

11. Why do people usually not wear the same kind of clothes all the time?

Exercise 4: Review Vocabulary

☐☐ Put these words in four groups.

**cotton   style   the globe   fashion   jeans   design   wool   sarong
the world   kimono   animal skin   international**

The History of the Bathing Suit

⟨ **Listening Activity 2** ⟩

Exercise 1: Get Ready to Listen

☐☐ Read these questions aloud with a partner. What do you think this story will be about?

1. A swimsuit and a bathing suit are the same thing.   True (**T**) or False (**F**)?

2. A bathing suit fits:
   a) in a bag
   b) under your clothes
   c) close to the body

3. Bikinis are for swimming at the beach.   **T F**

4. Before the 1800s, swimming was a popular form of recreation.   **T F**

5. The first bathing suits:
   a) were easy to swim in
   b) looked like street clothes
   c) were made of cotton

6. What are some things that women in the 1800s wore for swimming?
   a) wool bathing suits
   b) bikinis
   c) long pants
   d) shorts
   e) long skirts

f) long sleeves

g) stockings

h) high necklines

i) bathing caps

j) bathing slippers

k) T-shirts

7. What was the problem when women's bathing suits got wet?

8. Which things did men in the 1800s wear for swimming?

a) socks

b) shorts

c) tops

d) sweaters

e) pants

f) hats

9. Women's bathing suits got smaller and lighter for 19 years. **T F**

10. Today men wear tops with their bathing suits. **T F**

11. A bikini is a long bathing suit. **T F**

Exercise 2: Listen for Meaning

Listen to the story. What are some things it talks about?

Exercise 3: Listen for Details

Go back to the questions in Exercise 1. While you listen, answer the questions.

Exercise 4: Tell the Story

Tell the story of bathing suits to your partner. Use your own words. Then your partner will tell you the story.

| **Did You Know?** | A good way to find out what people in Canada wear to work or school is to look at advertisements in major newspapers. You can also find out what kind of clothes to wear in different seasons, and how much the clothes cost. |

Exercise 5: Write the Story

Write about the history of bathing suits.

International Styles

Exercise 1: Get Ready

☐☐ Work with a partner. Match the style and the country.

beret	Mexico
kimono	Scotland
sombrero	Afghanistan
sari	Japan
jeans	Morocco
fez	Germany
kaftan	the United States
anorak	France
kilt	Canada
sarong	Tahiti
lederhosen	India

Exercise 2: Complete the Paragraph

Choose the correct word for each space.

jeans   regions   clothes   people   women

Canadians don't have a national dress, but there are special _____ that people
1

wear in different _____ for traditional occasions. For example, in some parts
2

of Nova Scotia, men and _____ wear kilts. _____ in Alberta sometimes wear
3   4

western clothing, such as _____ and cowboy boots, at special events. At the
5

Quebec Winter Carnival people wear the costumes of the early French

pioneers.

Buying Clothes

> **Listening Activity 3**

Exercise 1: Get Ready to Listen

☐ ☐   Read the questions aloud with a partner. What do you think this conversation
will be about?

1. How many times does the sales clerk ask
    the question, "Can I help you?"

    a) once

    b) twice

    c) three times

2. What does the customer want to buy?

    a) a winter coat

    b) a business suit

    c) a ski outfit

3. What colour is she looking for?

    a) blue

    b) white

    c) grey

4. The suit has:
   a) a jacket
   b) pants
   c) a blouse

5. The customer takes:
   a) size 6
   b) size 8
   c) size 10

6. What is the other thing that the customer wants to buy?
   a) a skirt
   b) a jacket
   c) a blouse

7. What colours does the sales clerk suggest?
   a) white
   b) blue
   c) pink

8. Where is the mirror?
   a) on the wall
   b) near the elevator
   c) in the fitting room

9. How much does the suit cost?
   a) $220
   b) $235
   c) $35

10. The customer thinks that this is:
    a) a good price to pay
    b) a little expensive
    c) too much money to pay

11. How does the customer pay?
    a) with a cheque
    b) in cash
    c) by credit card

[○ ○] Exercise 2: Listen for Meaning

Listen to the conversation. What is it about?

[○ ○] Exercise 3: Listen for Details

Go back to the questions in Exercise 1. While you listen, answer the questions.

[○ ○] Exercise 4: Listen Again for Details

Discuss who said these things. Then listen again to check your answers.

1. Can I help you?   **sales clerk   customer**
2. I'm just browsing.   **sales clerk   customer**
3. What do you have in mind?   **sales clerk   customer**
4. Do you want to try it on?   **sales clerk   customer**
5. The fitting room is over here.   **sales clerk   customer**
6. Does it fit?   **sales clerk   customer**
7. The price tag is not clear.   **sales clerk   customer**
8. Will that be cash or charge?   **sales clerk   customer**

A Special Outfit

Role Play

Partner A

You are a customer. You go to a store to buy a new outfit for a party. Tell the sales clerk what kind of outfit you are looking for. Talk about size, colour, etc.

Partner B

You are a sales clerk in a store. Ask the customer about the outfit he or she is looking for. Ask about colour, size, etc. Offer some suggestions.

Both Partners

Write a dialogue. Be prepared to perform it for the class.

What About You?

Discuss these questions in a group.

1. What kind of clothes do you wear to work or class?
2. What kind of clothes do you like to wear when you relax?
3. What kind of clothes do you like to wear when you go out in the evening?
4. Do you ever buy fashion magazines? Which ones?
5. Do you have a special colour that you like to wear? What is it?
6. Do you have a special store where you buy clothes?
7. How often do you buy new clothes?

The Fashion Quiz: Answers

Exercise 2: Read for Information

Read the information, then check your answers from page 9.

1. The first people to wear blue jeans were miners. This was during the San Francisco gold rush in the 1850s. A man named Levi Strauss made pants out of heavy material for the miners. These were the first jeans.

2. The first kind of shoes that people wore were sandals. They were worn by the ancient Egyptians and later by the Greeks. Sandals were useful in hot climates because they protected the bottoms of the feet from hot sand.

3. The next kind of shoe, which people wore after sandals, was made from soft pieces of leather. The leather was tied around the ankle. The Romans, around 200 BC, were the first people to have professional shoemakers. The shoemakers made shoes especially for the right and left feet.

4. The bikini was designed in France in 1946. This was just after the United States tested a bomb near the islands of Bikini Atoll in the Pacific Ocean. A Parisian clothing designer wanted everyone to notice his new two-piece swimsuit. He called it a bikini. More people talked about his bikini than about the bomb!

5. Men started wearing long pants around 1800. Before that, only working men wore long pants. Rich men wore knee-length pants over stockings.

6. Buttons were first used as decoration on clothing and as jewellery. This was because people had buttons on their clothes, but no buttonholes!

7. Cotton is a natural fibre that comes from a plant. Silk and wool are also natural fibres, but they come from animals. Silk comes from a silk worm. We get wool from sheep.

8. Today, many teenagers wear jeans, T-shirts and leather jackets. In the 1960s, teenagers in North America, also wore jeans. The jeans were wide at the bottom, so they were called bell-bottoms. Many teenagers, especially boys, let their hair grow long. Teenagers also wore sandals and beads.

9. Gloves were made of linen and other materials in Ancient Egypt, around 1500 BC, but the oldest gloves ever found are about 10 000 years old. They were made from animal skins and were used to protect the hands from the cold. Actually, the gloves were more like mittens, because they didn't have individual fingers.

10. It's true! In the 1600s in Europe, men wore silk stockings and high-heeled shoes with lots of bows.

11. In western countries, men usually wear pants. For special occasions, Scottish men wear knee-length skirts called kilts. The guards at the Greek parliament also wear kilts.

12. A tuxedo is a suit that men wear to formal occasions, such as weddings. This suit is usually black, but sometimes men wear white tuxedo jackets with black pants.

Unit 3

Up in the Air

Hot-Air Balloons

Use these words to complete the paragraph.

tried   heated   went   changed   looked

Humans have always dreamed of flying. People _____ at birds and
$\overline{}_{1}$

wanted to build flying machines. None of the things people _____
$\overline{}_{2}$

were a success before hot-air balloons. With hot-air balloons,

people could go up in the air like birds for the first time.

The first hot-air balloons were made of paper or fabric. When the

balloon had hot air inside, it _____ up into the sky. When the air inside the
$\overline{}_{3}$

balloon was not _____, the balloon came down slowly. Today the materials
$\overline{}_{4}$

have _____ but the idea is the same, and people still like to go up in hot-air
$\overline{}_{5}$

balloons.

How Ballooning Began

> **Listening Activity 4**

Exercise 1: Get Ready to Listen

Work in a group. Discuss these questions.

1. What is a hot-air balloon made of?
2. When was the first successful
    hot-air balloon flight?
3. Will smoke make a hot-air balloon
    rise?
4. Can a hot-air balloon explode?

Exercise 2: Listen for Meaning

Listen to the story. What is the story about?

Exercise 3: Listen for Details

Read the questions aloud with a partner. Then, while you listen, answer the questions.

1.   What did the Montgolfier brothers make in their factory?
2.   What was their balloon made of?
3.   How far did their first balloon fly?
4.   What was the circumference of their second balloon?
5.   What was the date of their second try?
6.   How did people in the crowd react?
7.   What three animals went up in the third balloon?
8.   What country was Alberto Santos-Dumont from?
9.   Where did the first dirigible get caught?
10.   What was Santos-Dumont doing in the tree?
11.   What happened to the balloon after he jumped out?
12.   How far did he fly on his second flight?

Exercise 4: Tell the Story

Tell the story to your partner. Use your own words. Then your partner will tell you the story.

Exercise 5: Write the Story

Write the story of how ballooning began.

Balloon over Kenya

Exercise 1: Get Ready to Read

Work with a partner to find these animals on page 23.

buffalo	antelope	lion	hippo
zebra	elephant	goats	cattle

Exercise 2: Read Quickly to Increase Speed

Work with a partner. Read one paragraph at a time. After each paragraph, stop and discuss the questions on page 24.

Balloon over Kenya

A. The Masai Game Sanctuary in Kenya is one of the last places to see the wild animals of East Africa. At the game sanctuary you can see exotic animals such as buffalo, zebra, antelope and lions. For tourists who are afraid to go too close to the wild animals, there is a new way to see them. Tourists can observe the animals from a hot-air balloon.

B. The Governor's Camp Resort in Kenya owns a wonderful balloon. It is 27 meters high. This balloon is one of the four largest hot-air balloons in the world. The balloon can carry 10 passengers, the captain and the crew. The crew are from the Masai people. When they are not working on the balloon, they look after goats and cattle.

C. Tourists can watch the animals while the balloon is floating over the land. Most of the tourists are Americans. They pay $200 for a trip. When they are at the Governor's Camp, the tourists sleep in tents. But these tents are special. They are luxury tents. The tourists eat four-course meals. At night, elephants and hippos walk through the camp.

D. Often tourists take the balloon ride in the early morning. They float over plains and rivers watching the animals below. They can see elephants, lions and zebra in safety. Afterwards the balloon lands so that the passengers can have breakfast. Breakfast is often sausages, eggs and bacon, which are cooked on the balloon's burners. Often champagne is served with breakfast. Then the passengers are off again to see the animals in the wild.

Paragraph A

1. Where is the Masai Game Sanctuary?
2. Name some exotic animals that you can see there.
3. What are some tourists afraid of?
4. What is a new way to see the animals?

Paragraph B

5. How high is the balloon?
6. What is special about the balloon?
7. How many passengers can the balloon carry?
8. Who are the crew?
9. What is their usual job?

Paragraph C

10. Where do the tourists come from?
11. How much does a trip in the balloon cost?
12. Where do visitors to the Governor's Camp Resort sleep?
13. What kind of meals do they have in the camp?
14. What happens in the camp at night?

Paragraph D

15. What are some things tourists can see below them?
16. Why does the balloon sometimes land?
17. Describe breakfast.
18. How is the food cooked?
19. What happens after breakfast?

Exercise 3: Read Carefully for Details

Read the text again. Write the answers to the questions.

Exercise 4: Review Vocabulary

Put these words into five groups.

plains **watch** **eggs** **rivers** **tourists** **see** **crew** **goats**
Masai **land** **hippos** **bacon** **observe** **cattle** **sausages**

The History of Flight

Listen for the dates. Write the numbers that you hear.

In ____ the first hot-air balloon went up in the air over France. The
1
Montgolfier brothers invented the balloon, which stayed up for ten minutes

before it fell down.

Two years later, in ____, the parachute was
2
invented in France. Then the first dirigible, a

balloon powered by steam, was built in ____.
3
It travelled between Paris and a small village

in France.

In ____ the first gliders were built. Then,
4
starting in ____ in Germany, thousands of
5
gliders were built.

The Wright brothers studied the gliders, and built their own flying machines

with engines. In ____ they went to Kitty Hawk and tried to fly. Finally, they
6
were successful.

Between ____ and ____ Ferdinand von Zeppelin operated the first
7   8
commercial air service. In ____ an English company started regular
9
passenger flights between London and Paris.

On May 20, ____ Charles Lindberg made the first trip across the Atlantic
10
Ocean.

Unit 4

Apples and Corn Cobs

The Apple Quiz

Exercise 1: Get Ready

What do you know about apples? Do this quiz and find out. Discuss these questions in a group. More than one answer can be correct.

When you have finished, turn to page 36. Read the information to check your answers.

1. The shape of an apple is:
   a) square
   b) triangular
   c) round

2. Apples can be:
   a) red
   b) orange
   c) yellow

3. How many different kinds of apples are there?
   a) 500
   b) 2000
   c) 7000

4. Apples are good for your:
   a) teeth
   b) skin
   c) bones

5. Which vitamins are in apples?
   a) vitamin A
   b) vitamin B_6
   c) vitamin C

6. Which animals like apples?
   a) horses
   b) gorillas
   c) worms

7. How many calories are there in a medium-sized apple?
   a) 50
   b) 75
   c) 90

8. What percentage of an apple is water?
   a) 20 percent
   b) 55 percent
   c) 85 percent

9. What drinks can you make from apples?
   a) apple juice
   b) apple cider
   c) apple milk

10. The world's biggest apple weighed:
    a) 500 grams
    b) one kilogram
    c) one and a half kilograms

11. How many bushels of apples are sold each year in Canada?
    a) 10 million
    b) 25 million
    c) 50 million

12. Which city is called the "Big Apple"?

a) Calgary

b) Paris

c) New York

13. Apples grow in:

a) Canada

b) Norway

c) Japan

14. Apples are ready to pick:

a) in spring

b) in summer

c) in fall

15. Which weather conditions are good for growing apples?

a) lots of sunshine

b) a little cold weather

c) lots of rain

How Apples Came to Canada

 Exercise 1: Read Quickly for General Ideas

How Apples Came to Canada

When immigrants leave their countries they take many things with them. They take their languages, their customs and their own foods. Apples came to Canada from the north of France. This is how it happened.

When French people came to Canada, many of them settled in Port Royal. Today this place is called Annapolis, Nova Scotia. The settlers planted a few apple trees. That was in 1610. By 1700, there were more than a thousand apple trees in the Annapolis Valley.

When the pioneers settled in Canada, they faced long, harsh winters. They could not grow fresh fruits and vegetables. There were no refrigerators or supermarkets where they could buy what they needed. The only way to have fruits and vegetables during the long winter months was to dry and preserve what they had from the summer.

Apples were one of the most important foods for the settlers. When they gathered their apples in the early autumn, they used the fresh fruit to make juice, cider, apple butter and apple vinegar. They also used apples to feed their pigs, horses and cows. And, of course, everyone loved apple pie!

Later in the fall, the settlers dried apples so they would be able to eat them all winter. This was a special time. After all the apples were picked, everyone — mothers, fathers, children, grandparents and neighbours — got together for an

Did You Know?   Apples have so many vitamins that people often say, "An apple a day keeps the doctor away."

apple-drying party. They called this party an apple-picking bee. It was a chance to celebrate the apple harvest with music and dancing. All day long they worked on the apples. First they peeled the apples. Then they took out the cores. Next, they sliced the apples. Last, they dried the apples. After this, they had enough fruit for the winter.

The settlers used apples and the wood from apple trees in other ways as well. They made dolls from dried apples and they used the wood from the apple trees to make furniture and toys for their children. Then they burned the roots of the apple tree as fuel to keep warm and to cook their food.

Exercise 2: Read Carefully for Details

Work with a partner. Look in the text for the answers.

1. Name three things that people bring with them to a new country.
2. Where did French settlers first plant apple trees in Canada?
3. How many apple trees were there by 1700?
4. What problems did the pioneers have in the winter?
5. How did the pioneers get fruits and vegetables?
6. List some foods and drinks that were made from apples.

7. Which animals ate apples?

8. Give some information about the apple-drying party.

    a) When was it?

    b) Who was there?

    c) What was it called?

    d) Why was it special?

    e) How long did it last?

9. a) Write out the four steps that the settlers used to preserve apples.

    b) Match each step to a picture.

10. What were some of the ways to use these things?

    a) dried apples

    b) wood from the trees

    c) roots of apple trees

Did You Know?

People once believed that you could learn the name of your true love from an apple. People turned the stem and said the letters of the alphabet. The letter that they were saying when the stem broke would be the first letter of their true love's name.

How to Eat an Apple

Take an apple in your hand, open your mouth and bite. That is the best way to eat an apple. When you cook or peel an apple, some of the vitamins are lost. When you drink apple juice, you also get less vitamin A. For this reason, it is best to eat an apple raw. Be sure to wash it well first.

McIntosh Apples

Choose the correct word for each space.

forest   apples   red   trees   garden

McIntosh apples are very popular. They are a bright _____ colour. They taste
                                                        1

sweet and juicy. You can find them in most stores and supermarkets in

Canada.

McIntosh apples are named after a farmer in Ontario. In 1880 John McIntosh

found some apple trees growing in the _____. He planted the trees in his
                                       2

_____. Unfortunately, most of the _____ had soft, bitter fruit, but one tree
3   **4**

had delicious, crisp red apples.

John McIntosh began to grow more of this kind of tree in his garden. Soon his

_____ became famous. People began to call them McIntosh apples.
5

How Does an Apple Taste?

Here are some words to describe apples. Some of these words describe how apples look. This is called their **appearance**. Some words describe how apples feel when you bite into them. This is called the **texture** of the apple. Some words describe the way apples taste.

Make a chart. Put the words into the categories **appearance**, **taste**, or **texture**.

**crisp   juicy   red   round   sweet   dry   sour   hard   oval   crunchy
mushy   green   bitter   plump   soft   yellow**

Appearance	Taste	Texture
plump	sour	mushy

Indian Corn

Listening Activity 5

Exercise 1: Get Ready to Listen

A. Discuss these questions in a group.

1. Do you know another word for corn?
2. What are some ways to eat corn?
3. What are some countries that grow corn?
4. What are some foods you can make from corn?
5. These are some food products from corn that people eat in Canada. Match the food to the way we use the corn product.

cornflakes	as a vegetable
corn oil	as a snack at the movies
corn flour	as a breakfast cereal
popcorn	for frying food
corn on the cob	to make bread
corn nibblets	as a vegetable you eat with your hands

6. What do you put on corn on the cob?

B. Read the questions aloud with a partner. What do you think this story is about?

1. Who thinks that corn on the cob is a special treat?
   a) bankers
   b) children
   c) farmers

2. What do people like to put on corn on the cob?
   a) butter
   b) salt
   c) sugar

3. What is made from corn flour?
   a) powder
   b) ingredients
   c) bread

4. Agriculture began in:
   a) southern Canada
   b) Central Asia
   c) southern Mexico

5. Before they grew food, the Mayas:
   a) made bread
   b) hunted animals
   c) told stories

6. Agriculture began about:
   a) 1500 BC
   b) 2000 BC
   c) 3000 BC

7. How did farming change the Mayas' lifestyle?

   a) they hunted animals

   b) they built cities

   c) they gathered food

8. The idea of growing corn spread north:

   a) because of trade

   b) because animals liked the corn

   c) because people wanted popcorn

9. When did Europeans learn about corn?

   a) when they crossed the Atlantic Ocean

   b) when it was Thanksgiving

   c) before the 16th century

10. At the Thanksgiving holiday people:

   a) decorate the dining table

   b) make popcorn for fun

   c) swim in the ocean

Exercise 2: Listen for Meaning

Listen to the story. What is the story about?

Exercise 3: Listen for Details

Go back to the questions in Exercise 1. While you listen, choose the correct answers.

Exercise 4: Tell the Story

Tell the story of Indian corn to your partner. Use your own words. Then your partner will tell you the story.

Exercise 5: Write the Story

Write everything you remember about Indian corn.

How to Eat Corn on the Cob

First you put the cob in boiling water to cook. Second, you dry the corn. Then you roll the hot corn in butter. Next you add salt. Finally you pick the corn up and bite into it. Eating corn on the cob can be messy, but the taste is delicious. Yum!

The Story of Popcorn

Exercise 1: Get Ready to Read

What do you know about popcorn? Read these questions with a partner. Answer **T** (true) or **F** (false).

1. People like to eat popcorn with butter.
2. Popcorn was invented in this century.
3. You can only pop corn that has water in it.
4. Corn begins to steam after it pops.
5. Popcorn is yellow.
6. The English settlers taught the Native peoples how to pop corn.
7. A popcorn machine was invented in the 16th century.
8. Popcorn is good for you.

Exercise 2: Read Quickly to Check Your Predictions

Read the text quickly to find the answers to the questions. Change false information in Exercise 1 to true.

The Story of Popcorn

Popcorn is good to eat when it is hot. People like to eat it with butter and salt on it. You put popcorn in a bowl. Then you eat it with your fingers.

Today it is an American tradition to eat popcorn at the movies. Many people in Canada follow this tradition of eating popcorn at the movies too. The movies are new. They began as a form of entertainment only in this century. The story of popcorn is much older. In fact, it is 5000 years old.

5000 years ago the Native peoples of America discovered that some corn was good for popping. These peoples had three kinds of corn. Sweet corn was good to eat. Field corn was good for animals to eat. The corn sometimes called "Indian corn" was good for popping. In order to be good for popping, corn needs at least 14 percent water in it. It needs water because, when the corn is heated, the water turns to steam. The steam causes the corn to explode. In old English, the word "pop" was used to mean "explode." When corn explodes or pops, it becomes white and puffy. Then it is ready to eat.

In the 17th century, settlers who came to America learned about popcorn from the Native peoples. Popcorn was a popular dish. Actually, some Native peoples did not use popcorn only for food. They made necklaces out of stringed popcorn. They wore these necklaces at religious ceremonies.

Popping corn became more popular in the 19th century when someone invented a corn-popping machine. This machine made it easy to pop corn. In movie theatres across Canada and the United States, people started to order popcorn. By 1950, 85 percent of movie theatres sold popcorn. Today, popcorn is sold everywhere. Many video stores sell fresh popcorn, so you can eat popcorn even while you watch a movie at home.

The average person in North America eats two pounds of popcorn a year. People continue to like popcorn for three reasons. It is cheap, it is healthy, and it tastes delicious.

 ## Exercise 3: Read Carefully for Details

Work with a partner. Look for the answers in the text.

1. Name two things people like to put on popcorn.
2. Name a place where North Americans like to eat popcorn.
3. Who first discovered that corn was good for popping?
4. Make a chart. Write the three kinds of popcorn the Native peoples had and what each kind of corn was used for.

	Name of corn	Use
1.		
2.		
3.		

5. How much water does corn need, to be good for popping?
6. Explain how corn pops.
7. Name two ways that the Native peoples used popcorn in the 17th century.
8. Why did popcorn become popular in the 19th century?
9. Name two places that sell popcorn for people to eat while they watch a movie.
10. Give three reasons why people like popcorn.

The Apple Quiz: Answers

Exercise 2: Read for Information

Read the information. Check your answers from page 27.

1. The shape of an apple is round. Some apples have five bumps on the bottom. These apples are called "delicious" apples.

2. Apples come in different colours. Many of the apples we see in stores are red. Green and yellow apples are also popular.

3. There are more than 7000 different kinds of apples in the world. Many of these grow in North America. Most of the varieties are found in home gardens. Markets usually sell four or five favourite kinds, such as McIntosh and Delicious.

4. Apples have vitamins and minerals, so they are good for your skin, teeth and bones!

5. Apples contain vitamins A, B_1, B_2, B_3, B_6, B_{12}, C, E and folic acid. They also have several minerals.

6. Wild animals eat whatever food is available. Animals in zoos like to eat apples as a treat. They are a favourite fruit of gorillas. People also give them to their horses. Worms like to eat apples too, from the inside!

7. A medium-sized apple has about 75 calories.

8. If you are thirsty, eat an apple. A fresh, raw apple contains about 85 percent water. This is equal to about half a glass of water!

9. Apple juice and apple cider are popular drinks made from apples. Cider vinegar is also made from apples. It was used by the pioneers for pickling, to preserve fruits and vegetables.

10. The world's largest apple was found in England. It weighed 1.357 kilograms. That is as big as most bags of apples.

11. About 25 million bushels of apples are produced each year in Canada.

12. New York is called the "Big Apple." It got its name when people at the New York Convention and Visitors Bureau decided to promote New York as a "new and brightly polished" place. They said that for sports heroes and entertainers, there are many apples on the tree. This means there are many cities where they can perform. To perform in New York, however, is to play the "Big Apple."

13. Apples grow in many countries in the world. They grow as far north as Sweden and Norway. They also grow in Australia, New Zealand, Argentina, Japan and many other places. Canada and the United States are big apple producers.

14. Apple trees bloom in late spring. At this time, the flowers and fruit are not harmed by frost. The apples are ready to pick in the fall.

15. Apples grow well in many parts of North America because the weather conditions are right. Apples need a lot of sunshine, a little cold weather in the winter, good soil and a little wind. If there is too much rain, the apple tree will die. Apple trees die if their roots are always wet. Apples also grow in Norway and Japan, which are northern countries.

Farming

Different Kinds of Farms

Exercise 1: Get Ready to Read

Discuss these questions in a group.

1. What is a farm?
2. Name some animals that you find on a farm.
3. Name some foods that come from a farm.
4. What other products do we get from a farm?
5. What happens on the farm in winter? In summer?
6. What machines are used on the farm?

Exercise 2: Read Quickly for General Ideas

Different Kinds of Farms

Many people all over the world work on farms. A farm is a place where people grow plants and raise animals for food. Farmers grow food for themselves and for others to eat.

In many traditional cultures, almost everyone farms the land. Families have farms on a small piece of land. The family produces only enough food to feed itself. People do not have many machines, and they work very hard. In industrial cultures, there are not as many farmers, but the farmers have more land. Wheat farms in Canada can be one million hectares. The farmers use machines to make their work easier and faster. These farms produce food for many people. The food goes to markets and stores all over the country.

Most farmers grow plants, called crops, which they harvest. The most important crops are the cereals. These are plants that look like tall grasses. They produce seeds, called grain. In North America and Europe, wheat is the most important grain. In other parts of the world, rice is more important. Grains such as wheat are made into flour and then baked into bread. Corn, oats and barley are other cereals. They can also be made into flour, but they are often used to feed farm animals.

Farmers in North America grow other crops, such as vegetables and fruits. Some vegetables, such as lettuce and cauliflower, go to the market for people to buy. Other vegetables are used to feed farm animals. Potatoes are an important food for people in Canada and in many other parts of the world. Carrots are an example of a food that is eaten by people and by farm animals too.

Fruits such as apples, peaches and plums grow in orchards in Canada and the United States. Different kind of fruits grow in different places because of climate. In the southern United States, farmers can grow oranges and grapefruit because it is warm. In Canada the climate is cooler. Apples and pears grow well here.

Many farmers also keep animals. Dairy farms are farms where cows are kept for milk. The milk is sold for people to drink. It is also made into other dairy products such as cheese, butter and yoghurt.

Ranches are farms where animals such as cows and sheep are kept for their meat. We get other products from animals on the farm as well. Some examples are eggs from chickens and wool from sheep.

Large farms in North America have machines to do many jobs. These machines make farming easier and help the farmer produce more food. The tractor is the most important machine because it pulls other machines. Planters are machines that plant seeds. Harvesters are machines that harvest, or pick the crops.

📖 Exercise 3: Read Carefully for Details

Work with a partner. Look in the text for the answers.

1. What is a farm?
2. How are farms different in traditional cultures and industrial cultures? Complete the chart.

	Traditional cultures	Industrial cultures
size of land		
amount of food		
machines		

3. What are crops?
4. What are the most important crops?
5. Give the following information about cereals:
   a) What do they look like?
   b) What are the seeds called?
   c) Which are the most important grains?
6. What is wheat made into?
7. List some other cereals. What are they used for?
8. Give two uses for vegetables.
9. Give an example of an important vegetable for:
   a) people
   b) people and animals
10. What do we call the farms where we grow fruit?
11. Why can't farmers grow oranges in Canada?
12. Give examples of fruits that grow well in Canada.
13. What are dairy farms?
14. What are some dairy products?
15. What are ranches?
16. Give two examples of other products from the farm. What animal does each one come from?

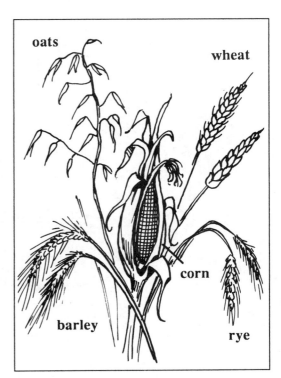

Product	Animal

17. Give two reasons why farmers in North America use machines.

18. Which machine is the most important? Why?

19. What do other machines do?

Exercise 4: Review Vocabulary

Make a chart similar to the one below. Put these words into the categories on the chart.

oats   milk   corn   wheat   cheese   butter

tractor   carrot   barley   wool   orange   yoghurt

chicken   pork   harvester   apple   beef   plum

cauliflower   eggs   rice   potato   lamb   pear

lettuce   planter

Cereal	Dairy Product	Meat	Fruit or Vegetable	Machine	Other

From Moo to You

> Listening Activity 6

Exercise 1: Get Ready to Listen

□ □   A. Look at the picture on page 43. Work with a partner to find the following:

pipeline   glass recording jar   glass-lined tank   pump

B. Read the questions aloud with a partner. What do you think the information is about?

1. How much milk can a cow give in ten months?

2. How often are cows milked?

3. Where does the cow go to be milked?

4. What is used to milk a cow?

5. Why is the glass jar marked?

6. What happens to the milk in the tank?

7. Why is milk pasteurized?

8. What temperature is needed to pasteurize milk?

9. Why is milk homogenized?

10. Name three kind of containers that milk is put into.

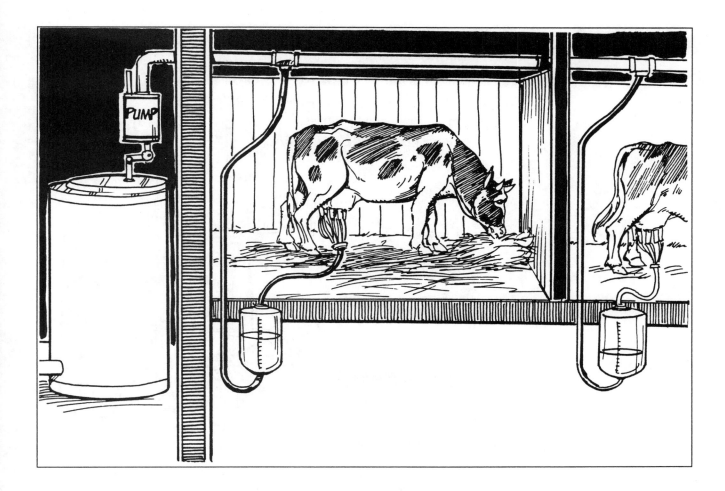

○○   **Exercise 2:   Listen for Meaning**

Listen to the information. What is the information about?

○○   **Exercise 3:   Listen for Details**

Go back to the questions in Exercise 1. While you listen, answer the questions.

Exercise 4: Review Information

 Work with a partner to put these steps in the correct order.

    a. The milk is taken to stores.

    b. The milk is homogenized.

    c. The cow goes into the barn to be milked.

    d. The milk is put into bottles, cartons or plastic bags.

    e. The milk is pasteurized.

    f. People buy the milk.

    g. A milking machine milks the cow.

    h. A pipeline takes the milk to a glass recording jar.

    i. The milk is pumped to a glass-lined tank.

    j. A tanker takes the milk to the dairy.

Did You Know?	In cities and towns across Canada, it is illegal to raise animals such as chickens for food. Also, city animals such as pigeons or squirrels cannot be eaten. This is for reasons of public health. City animals may be unhealthy because they often eat leftover food from people's garbage cans. The animals may be affected by pollution as well.

Farming

> **Video Activity 1: Part 1**

Exercise 1: Discuss

Discuss these questions in a group.

1. What are some different kinds of farms?
2. What are some products we get from those farms?
3. Name some steps farmers go through to grow crops.
4. How do the farmers' crops come to us?
5. Describe some machines that are used on farms in North America to plant, to harvest and to milk.
6. Give some examples of dairy products.

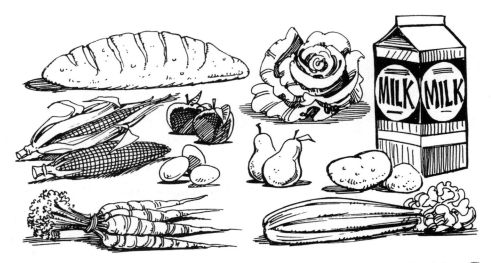

Metropolitan Separate School Board
Continuing Education Dept.
ADULT ENGLISH CLASSES

Exercise 2: Get Ready to Watch the Video

Read the questions aloud with a partner.

1. What are some things that farmers grow or raise on their farms?
2. Agriculture means raising crops and animals for food. **T** (true) or **F** (false)?
3. List six things that we can buy in the market.
4. Where do farmers keep their cows in winter?
5. At what time of year are many animals born?

6. What does the calf do after it is born?

7. How often are cows milked?

8. What is pasteurization?

   a) putting cows in the field

   b) heating milk to kill bacteria

   c) using a machine to milk cows

9. Give four examples of dairy products.

10. What is a greenhouse?

11. Name four things that plants need in order to grow.

12. Why do farmers plough and cultivate the soil?

13. Farmers put chemicals on seeds after they plant them. **T F**

14. Corn is planted by hand. **T F**

15. With good soil, sun and water, corn grows quickly. **T F**

16. The corn we see is for:

    a) animals

    b) people

17. The machine used to plant vegetables is called a _____.

Exercise 3: Watch the Video for General Ideas

Watch the video. What are some topics that are discussed?

Exercise 4: Watch the Video for Details

Go back to the questions in Exercise 2. While you watch the video, answer the questions.

Pronunciation

The stress in English words is not on the same syllable in each word.

These words have the primary stress on the first syllable.

animal

harvest

Europe

vegetables

chicken

country

problem

These words have the primary stress on the second syllable.

machine

important

America

Japan

invented

Write the words. Then say the words after your teacher. Mark the stress as you say the words.

What Do Animals Say?

Work in a group. Match the animal with the sound it makes.

Example: People: blah, blah, blah

chirp   gobble   bow wow   moo   baa   cock-a-doodle-do   buzz

hiss   meow   oink   neigh   cluck   croak   quack   bleat   grrrr

cow	goat
horse	turkey
pig	bird
rooster	frog
dog	duck
cat	snake
chicken	bee
lamb	bear

Baby Animals

 Work with a partner. Find the name of the baby for each animal.

lamb   duckling   colt   fawn   piglet   kitten

chick   puppy   cub   calf   bunny

chicken	dog
deer	cow
cat	horse
sheep	bear
rabbit	duck

Farming

(**Video Activity 1: Part 2**)

Exercise 1: Discuss

 Discuss these questions in a group.

1. What kinds of fruit are grown in orchards?
2. Ranches are places where animals are raised for food. What are some animals you might find on a ranch?
3. What is the product we make from wheat?
4. Root vegetables grow under the ground. What are the names of some root vegetables?
5. Lettuce is harvested by machine.   **T** (true) or **F** (false)?
6. Apples are harvested by machine.   **T   F**

Exercise 2: Get Ready to Watch the Video

 Read the questions aloud with a partner.

1. Orchards are special farms where farmers grow fruits such as _____ , _____ and _____ .
2. Bees like the smell of flowers. **T** (true) or **F** (false)?
3. All fruit grows on trees. **T F**
4. In some places fruit can grow all year. **T F**
5. Ranches are places to raise _____ .
6. We get products from certain animals. Complete the chart.

Name of animal	Products we get
sheep	
goats	
pigs	
hens	

7. What colour are turkeys?
8. Giving water to plants in dry places is called _____ .
9. Name four root vegetables.
10. Lettuce must be _____ and _____ .
11. Who works to harvest lettuce?
12. Harvesting cauliflower is a big job. **T F**
13. The machine called the combine does _____ things.
14. Wheat is used for _____ , _____ and _____ .
15. What colour are pumpkins?
16. Apples are picked by machines. **T F**
17. What is controlled in a warehouse?
18. What foods do we see on the table at the end of the video?

 ## Exercise 3: Watch the Video for General Ideas

Watch the video. What are some topics that are discussed?

Exercise 4: Watch the Video for Details

Go back to the questions in Exercise 2. While you watch the video, answer the questions.

Unit 6

Fast Food

Do You Like Fast Food?
Interaction
Discussion

Pizza Pie
Interaction
Reading

Let's Order In
Listening Activity 7

Ordering Fast Food
Role Play

The Slowest Fast Food
Dictation

Chewing Gum
Reading

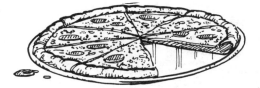

Do You Like Fast Food?

Exercise 1: Get Ready

Work in a group. Look at the picture. Find the foods that you eat or drink:

1. in a bun
2. with ketchup
3. hot
4. cold
5. with a straw
6. with onions
7. with your fingers
8. at the movies
9. as a meal
10. as a snack
11. from a bag
12. with a fork
13. with sauce
14. as a dessert
15. with a spoon
16. with salt

Exercise 2: Discuss

Discuss these questions in a group.

1. What is fast food?

2. Name as many fast foods as you can.

3. Why do we say "fast food"?

4. What is your favourite kind of fast food?

5. How often do you eat fast food?

6. What is your favourite fast-food restaurant?

7. What are some good things about fast food? Some bad things?

8. Name some fast foods that you eat as meals. Name some that you eat as snacks.

Pizza Pie

Exercise 1: Get Ready to Read

What do you know about pizza? Discuss these questions in a group.

1. How many pizzas are eaten in North America every year?

    a) a million

    b) a billion

    c) two billion

2. Pizza comes from:

    a) Germany

    b) Italy

    c) Spain

3. When was pizza first made?

    a) in the 1700s

    b) in the 1800s

    c) in the 1900s

4. The first pizzeria in North America was in:

    a) Toronto

    b) Chicago

    c) New York

5. Which topping is the most popular?

    a) cheese

    b) mushrooms

    c) pepperoni

Exercise 2: Read Quickly for General Ideas

Pizza Pie

Pizza is a fast-food favourite in many places. It's great because you can eat it alone, with the family or among a group of friends. Pizzas come in many sizes. You can eat pizza in different ways. You can eat a slice of pizza with a knife and fork, of course. But most people prefer to eat pizza with their hands. They say it tastes better that way. Pizza is also easy to get. It's easy to find, easy to order, fast to prepare and you can choose many different toppings to put on it.

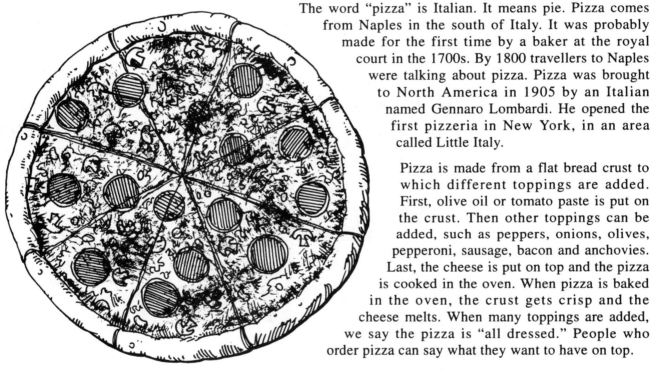

The word "pizza" is Italian. It means pie. Pizza comes from Naples in the south of Italy. It was probably made for the first time by a baker at the royal court in the 1700s. By 1800 travellers to Naples were talking about pizza. Pizza was brought to North America in 1905 by an Italian named Gennaro Lombardi. He opened the first pizzeria in New York, in an area called Little Italy.

Pizza is made from a flat bread crust to which different toppings are added. First, olive oil or tomato paste is put on the crust. Then other toppings can be added, such as peppers, onions, olives, pepperoni, sausage, bacon and anchovies. Last, the cheese is put on top and the pizza is cooked in the oven. When pizza is baked in the oven, the crust gets crisp and the cheese melts. When many toppings are added, we say the pizza is "all dressed." People who order pizza can say what they want to have on top.

Pizza isn't very expensive. It's a popular food to order when friends get together. Teammates can eat it together after a game. It tastes good after a movie or when you work late at the office. It can be a complete meal because it has a kind of bread, cheese or meat, and vegetables.

Today, North Americans consume almost two billion pizzas a year. The most popular topping is pepperoni, with extra cheese as the second most popular topping. Pizza will probably be around for a long time to come.

Exercise 3: Check Your Predictions

Go back to the questions. How many of your predictions were correct?

 ## Exercise 4: Read Carefully for Details

Work with a partner. Look in the text for the answers.

1. Describe how people like to eat pizza.
2. Give some of the ways to get a pizza.
3. What does the word "pizza" mean?
4. Who made the first pizza?
5. How long have people been talking about pizza?
6. Who brought pizza to North America?
7. Describe how to make pizza.
8. Name some toppings you can put on pizza.
9. Where do you cook pizza?
10. Give some examples of the times when people like to eat pizza.
11. Why can pizza be a complete meal?
12. Which toppings are the most popular?

Let's Order In

Listening Activity 7

Exercise 1: Get Ready to Listen

☐ ☐ **Cover Exercise 4 on page 57.**

Read the questions aloud with a partner. What do you think this conversation will be about?

1. What were the speakers doing that afternoon that made them so hungry?
2. What three kinds of food do they think of ordering in?
3. How much money does the speaker have?
4. What two things do they think are wrong with ordering Chinese food?
5. Why does the girl want to order pizza?
6. When is the pizza free?
7. What kind of pizza do they plan to order?
8. What does the girl not want on the pizza?
9. How much will the pizza cost?
10. Why don't they want the pizza place to hurry?

Exercise 2: Listen for Meaning

Listen to the conversation. Then answer these questions.

1. What is the conversation about?
2. How many people are talking?

Exercise 3: Listen for Details

Go back to the questions in Exercise 1. While you listen, answer the questions.

Exercise 4: Practise Speaking

Practise the conversation in a group of three.

Let's Order In

Tom:	Hey guys, I'm starving. Let's order in.
George:	Yes. That's a great idea. I'm hungry too, especially after the game we played this afternoon.
Gaby:	What shall we order: pizza, Chinese food, chicken?
Tom:	I like Chinese food but I only have five bucks on me. How much do you think it will come to?
George:	That depends what we order. What do you think, Gaby?
Gaby:	I think we should get pizza. Last time we ordered Chinese food. It was really good but it took ages. Pizza always comes fast.
Tom:	OK. Let's get pizza. What's that place called, the one where you get the pizza free if it takes more than half an hour?
George:	Free pizza. Great.
Gaby:	Not free, George. Not unless it takes more than half an hour.
George:	Well pizza's good anyway. What kind shall we order?
Tom:	How about all-dressed?
Gaby:	All-dressed is good but I don't like mushrooms. I hate the texture. Ask for an all-dressed without mushrooms.
George:	OK. I'll order one large pizza, all-dressed, hold the mushrooms. How much does it cost?
Tom:	About 12 bucks I think. That comes to $4 each, plus a tip. I think we have enough. I'll tell the pizza place to hurry.
Gaby:	No, don't tell them to hurry. If it takes them more than half an hour, the pizza is free (ha,ha,ha,ha).
George:	Yes, Tom. Tell them to take their time (ha,ha,ha).

Exercise 5: Review Expressions

Work with a partner. Find another way to say the following things.

1. I'm **hungry**.
2. I only have **$5**.
3. It took **a long time**.
4. How about a pizza **with everything on it**?
5. **Don't put** any mushrooms on the pizza.
6. The **total** cost is....
7. Tell them **not to hurry**.

Ordering Fast Food

Role Play

Partner A

You are a customer. You are calling to order food on the telephone. Choose the type of food you will order (pizza, Chinese, chicken, etc.). Call the restaurant and ask for information about the food you want. Ask about price, how long the delivery will take, etc. Ask for extras, such as ketchup, toppings for pizza, etc. Give your name, address and phone number.

Partner B

You work in a restaurant. A customer calls to order food. Give the customer information about the food. Ask if he or she wants extra cheese, onions, etc. Ask the customer for his or her name, address and telephone number. Write the information down.

Both Partners

Write a dialogue. Be prepared to perform it for the class.

Did You Know?   Ketchup comes from China. It began as a spicy sauce made of fish and mushrooms, called ke-tsiap. The recipe was brought to England by sailors. In England, tomatoes were added, and the name became ketchup.

The Slowest Fast Food

There is a fast-food restaurant in California where the service is very slow. It is slow because it is owned by two elderly sisters. One sister is 92 years old, and the other sister is 95 years old. One sister works while the other sister takes a nap. The two sisters move so slowly that it takes almost an hour to get a sandwich. Even a cup of coffee or a soft drink takes half an hour to come to the table.

Chewing Gum

Exercise 1: Get Ready to Read

Discuss these two questions in a group.

1. Why do you think people chew gum?
2. Why do some people not like the idea of chewing gum?

Exercise 2: Read Quickly for General Ideas

Read the text quickly. What is it about?

Chewing Gum

Chewing gum is very popular in the United States and Canada. People chew gum on the bus, in the streets and while they watch television. Young people like chewing gum so much that schools have regulations against chewing in class. Some people like a special kind of gum called bubble gum. They chew it for a while and then they blow bubbles with it. Chewing gum has a long history. It has changed in many ways over the past 100 years.

The story of gum begins in Mexico. Gum is made from the sap of a tree that grows in the jungles of Mexico. The name for this sap is chictli. An army general from Mexico brought some chictli to New York. A man named Thomas Adams was trying to make rubber. He thought he could make rubber from chictli so he bought a lot of the gum from the general. Unfortunately, Thomas Adams' plan to make rubber didn't work, but he discovered another thing to do with the chictli.

People at that time liked to chew wax. Thomas Adams noticed that his son liked to chew the chictli. The gum had no taste but it was still better than chewing wax. Adams began to market his product as chewing gum. He sold it as small "chickle balls," for a penny each. In 1875 a druggist had the idea of adding flavours to give the gum more taste. The druggist tried several different flavours. The most popular flavour was peppermint.

William Wrigley Jr., a soap salesman, was the first person to use modern processing and packaging for gum. He began advertising his gum, and it became very popular. Two gums that he introduced, Wrigley's Spearmint and Juicy Fruit, are still top-selling gums today.

A little later, two brothers, the Fleer brothers, became interested in gum. They added some new ingredients. Then one brother had a great idea. He put candy around the gum. This new kind of gum was called "Chicklets." The other brother found a gum that made bubbles. He called this discovery "Double Bubble." Both of these new kinds of gum were a success.

Today we can buy many kinds of gum. All sorts of people continue to chew gum, school children continue to blow bubbles in class, and schools continue to have regulations against chewing gum in class.

Exercise 3: Read Carefully for Details

Work with a partner. Look in the text for the answers.

1. What is chictli?
2. Where does it grow?
3. Why was Thomas Adams interested in chictli?
4. What did people chew in the past?
5. What gave Adams the idea of using chictli as chewing gum?
6. Who had the idea of adding flavour to the gum?
7. What was the most popular flavour?
8. What two things made Wrigley's gum successful?
9. Name two gums Wrigley sold.
10. What two ideas made the Fleer brothers successful?

Exercise 4: Review Details

Put these sentences in the correct order.

a. A druggist added flavour to gum.
b. Thomas Adams bought chictli from the general.
c. Adams began to sell gum to chew.
d. Schools have regulations against chewing gum.

e. A Mexican army general brought chictli to New York.

f. The Fleer brothers put candy around the gum.

g. Adam's son liked to chew the chictli gum.

h. Wrigley began to use modern processes and packaging for gum.

Exercise 5: Review Vocabulary

Match the words that go together.

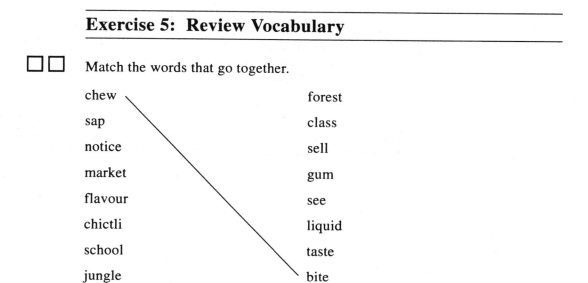

chew   forest

sap   class

notice   sell

market   gum

flavour   see

chictli   liquid

school   taste

jungle   bite

Exercise 6: Practise Pronunciation

Listen to the teacher read some expressions. Try to write exactly what you hear.

Unit 7

Money and Banking

Money Here, Money There

Discuss these questions in a group.

A. Look at some Canadian coins.

1. How many different coins are there?

2. How much is each coin worth?

3. Describe the animal or other pictures you see.

4. Who is the person on the back of each coin?

B. Look at some money that students have from other countries.

1. How many different coins does each country have?

2. How much is each coin worth?

3. Describe the pictures that you see.

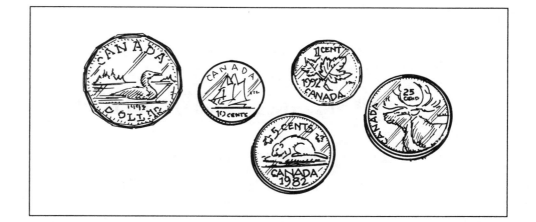

The History of Money

Exercise 1: Get Ready to Read

What do you know about money? Work in a group. Discuss these questions.

1. Before money people got things by:

   a) stealing

   b) working

   c) barter

2. The first metal used for money was:

   a) nickel

   b) gold

   c) brass

3. Which metal was not used as money?

    a) iron

    b) aluminum

    c) copper

4. In Canada, the loonie is made of:

    a) gold and brass

    b) iron and nickel

    c) nickel and bronze

5. What was never used as money?

    a) tea

    b) salt

    c) ink

6. Which of these things were used as money?

    a) feathers

    b) shells

    c) trees

Exercise 2: Read Quickly for General Ideas

The History of Money

A long time ago, people didn't have money. They traded things to get what they wanted. Suppose you had some chickens or a goat. Your friend had some vegetables and some grain. You could offer your friend three chickens or one goat for his food. If you could agree on the trade, you had a deal.

This system of trading things, called barter, worked pretty well for a long time. But what if your friend didn't want your animals? If you had something else you could use, something everyone agreed on, it would make trading easier. After a while, people started using special objects, called tokens, just for trade.

This was the beginning of money. In different countries, different things were used as tokens. Tokens were generally something unusual or something valuable. For example, in ancient Egypt, salt was very important. People traded blocks of salt for many things. In ancient China, tools were very important. People made small metal tools and traded them.

In some countries, the tokens were not valuable things. They were common objects. In Africa people traded stones and beads. Native peoples in the land that later became Canada used coloured beads and shells. In other places people traded whales' teeth, birds' feathers, and even tea leaves. Using tea leaves had an advantage, too. If you didn't spend your money, you could always pour hot water on it and drink it!

After a while, metal began to be used as money. Gold quickly became very popular for coins. It was popular for three reasons. First, it was hard to find, so it had a lot of value. Second, it was easy to shape into circles, so it was easy to use for making coins. Third, it stayed shiny for a long time, so it looked pretty. People in ancient Egypt used gold rings as money. In other places, people used metals that were easier to get. For example, people who lived near the Aegean Sea used copper. People in Great Britain used iron.

Today, in Canada, we use several metals to make our coins. Pennies are made of copper. Nickels are made of nickel, but may have some copper, brass or other metals too. Dimes and quarters are made of silver, mixed with other metals. Loonies are gold in colour, but are made from nickel covered with bronze.

Exercise 3: Read Carefully for Details

Work with a partner. Look in the text for the answers.

1. How did people get things before they had money?
2. What is this system called?
3. When did it not work?
4. What are tokens?
5. Why did people start using tokens?
6. Which objects were used as tokens
    a) in ancient Egypt?
    b) in China?
    c) in Africa?
7. What other objects were used?
8. What was first used for money?
9. Give three reasons why gold became popular.
10. Name some other metals used to make coins.
11. What metals are used today in Canada to make these coins?
    a) pennies
    b) nickels
    c) dimes
    d) quarters
    e) loonies

Did You Know?   The highest amount of money available today in one bill is from the United States. There is a $10 000 bill in the United States. The lowest amount printed is in Indonesia. It is the sen. It is worth a 10 000th of a penny.

Exercise 4: Check Your Answers

 Work with a partner. Go back to Exercise 1 and check your answers.

Saving Money

The words "saving money" are used in different ways in Canada. When bankers talk about saving money, they mean keeping money in the bank. But when stores talk about saving money, they mean that you can buy something at a lower price.

Money in the Bank

Exercise 1: Get Ready to Read

 Work with a partner to match the definitions.

1. a piece of paper you use to pay a bill	balance
2. to take money out of the bank	deposit
3. an account where you can save your money	interest
4. the money you keep in your account	withdraw
5. to put money in the bank	savings account
6. the extra money the bank gives you when you keep money there	cheque
7. the money you pay the bank when you write cheques	bank book
8. a book the bank gives you to tell you how much money you have	chequing account
9. a paper the bank sends you to tell you how much money you have	statement
10. an account where you can write cheques	service charge

Exercise 2: Read Quickly for General Ideas

Money in the Bank

Keeping your money in the bank is a good idea. Your money is safe, and you also make extra money called interest. Interest is the money the bank pays you for leaving your money there.

There are several different kinds of bank accounts, so it is important to know what kind of account is best for you. A savings account gives you the most interest. It is a good place to put money that you don't need to spend right away. When you open a savings account, you will get a bank book with your name and account number on it. When you deposit money or withdraw money, it will be marked in your bank book. Interest is usually paid to you monthly, but some savings accounts pay interest daily.

A chequing account does not have a bank book. It has cheques. The cheques have your name and address on them. They also have your account number on them. When you write cheques, the money comes out of your account. Writing cheques is useful for paying bills or when you do not want to carry a lot of cash (money) with you. You earn some interest in a chequing account, but not as much interest as in a savings account. You also have to pay a small amount every time you write a cheque. This is called a service charge.

With a chequing account you get a statement every month. A statement is a paper that tells you how much money you spent or put in your account that month. The money you keep in your account is called the balance.

Exercise 3: Read Carefully for Details

Work with a partner. Look in the text for the answers.

1. Give two reasons why keeping your money in the bank is a good idea.
2. What is interest?
3. What is one advantage of a savings account?
4. Which money should you put in a savings account?
5. How do you keep track of your money in a savings account?
6. How often is interest paid?
7. Name three things you find on a cheque.
8. Give two reasons it is useful to write cheques.
9. How much money do you earn in a chequing account?
10. What do you have to pay when you write a cheque?
11. What does a statement tell you?
12. What is a balance?

Changing Money

Exercise 1: Get Ready to Listen

☐☐ Read the questions aloud with a partner. What do you think the conversation will be about?

1. What does the man want to do?
2. Where is he going?
3. How much money does he want?
4. What is the exchange rate?
5. How much does it come to in Canadian money?
6. A few years ago it cost less. **T** (true) or **F** (false)?
7. The man wants to withdraw the money from his account. **T F**
8. What is his account number?
9. How much is the service charge?
10. What is the service charge for?
11. The man is happy to pay the service charge. **T F**
12. How many hundred-dollar bills does the man want?
13. The man says he wants to go shopping. **T F**

Did You Know?   Dollars are sometimes called bucks. This is because, in the past in North America, people traded deerskin, or buckskin. This was before they had money.

Exercise 2: Listen for Meaning

Listen to the conversation. What is the conversation about?

 Exercise 3: Listen for Details

Go back to the questions in Exercise 1. While you listen, answer the questions.

At the Bank

Role Play

Partner A

You are at the bank. You are a customer. Explain what you want to do at the bank (exchange money, cash a cheque, make a deposit, etc.).

Partner B

You are a teller at a bank. Help the customer make the transactions.

Both Partners

Write a dialogue. Be prepared to perform it for the class.

Did You Know?   Money is sometimes called "dough" or "bread." This makes sense, because if you have no money, you can't eat!

Unit 8

Spring

Migration of Animals
Interaction
Reading

About Animals
Number Dictation

Hibernation
Vocabulary

The Four Seasons: Spring
Video Activity 2: Part 1

The Four Seasons: Spring
Video Activity 2: Part 2

What About You?
Discussion
Writing

Migration of Animals

Exercise 1: Get Ready to Read

To migrate means to travel. There are many animals that migrate.

Discuss these questions in a group. Choose the best answers. Use the pictures to help you.

1. Which animals migrate?
   a) birds
   b) butterflies
   c) turtles
   d) bears

2. Animals migrate to:
   a) look for food
   b) escape from enemies
   c) see new places

3. Animals migrate:
   a) once a year
   b) twice a year
   c) every month

4. The longest trip made by an animal is:
   a) 10 000 kilometres
   b) 20 000 kilometres
   c) 40 000 kilometres

Exercise 2: Read Quickly for General Ideas

Migration of Animals

Many animals migrate from one place to another. We often notice the movement of birds because we see them leave in the fall and return in the spring. Some birds fly thousands of kilometres each year. Birds aren't the only animals that travel, however. Other animals such as whales, caribou and turtles travel too.

There are different reasons why animals travel. Animals sometimes eat all the food in an area, and must travel to search for more. The caribou is an example of an animal that migrates in search of food. The caribou is a large animal that lives in northern Canada and can travel as far as 480 kilometres to look for food. The caribou travel in large groups called herds. In the past there were many more caribou than there are today. Sometimes herds of up to a million caribou would cross a river together. In the Yukon, in northern Canada, they would stop the boats on the rivers for several days.

Many fish and animals migrate between fresh water and salt water, or to warmer oceans in the winter. Salmon are born upstream in rivers. They swim downstream, and spend their adult life in the ocean. When they are ready to lay their eggs, they return to the place where they were born. Humpback whales swim on regular routes between Canada and the United States. They spend their summers in the Arctic Ocean and their winters in the warm Pacific waters near California.

Many birds travel with the seasons. They live in Canada in the summer and travel south in the winter in search of the best climate in which to find food and have their babies. Some birds fly very far each year. For example, the North American golden plover breeds in the Canadian Arctic in the summer. In winter, it flies to South America — 3200 kilometres away. The longest journey is made by a small bird called the Arctic tern. It flies between the Arctic and the Antarctic Oceans every year.

Another creature that migrates from Canada is the butterfly. Few butterflies can survive the cold temperature of a northern winter. The monarch butterfly is a large reddish-brown butterfly that lives in Canada in summer and travels south to the United States and Mexico in winter. Monarch butterflies fly south in large groups — sometimes 10 000 at a time. Sometimes, when a large group of butterflies lands on some trees, the trees look reddish brown instead of green. The butterflies travel about 1400 kilometres round-trip, from Canada to California and Mexico in the winter and back again to Canada in summer.

Exercise 3: Read Carefully for Details

Work with a partner. Look in the text for the answers.

1. What does migration mean?
2. Give some examples of animals that migrate.
3. Give a reason why animals migrate.
4. Why do caribou travel?
5. Which animals stopped boats on the river in the past? Explain how they did it.
6. Where do fish and whales migrate?
7. Explain the migration route of salmon.
8. Where do humpback whales live in summer? In winter?
9. Give two reasons why birds fly south in winter.
10. Which bird makes the longest journey each year? How far does it fly?
11. Why do butterflies fly south in winter?
12. Give some information about the monarch butterfly.
    a) What does it look like?
    b) Where does it live?
    c) How big is its group?
    d) How long is its journey?

About Animals

Write the numbers that the teacher dictates.

1. The North American golden plover is a bird that flies _____ kilometres each year.
2. Another bird, the Arctic tern, flies _____ kilometres during migration.
3. The caribou's migration route is _____ kilometres long.
4. Monarch butterflies fly _____ kilometres annually.
5. When they migrate, monarch butterflies travel in groups of _____ .
6. The blue whale swims _____ kilometres each year during migration.
7. Grey whales swim _____ kilometres on their migration route.
8. The bat flies _____ kilometres round-trip from Labrador to Bermuda.
9. The Atlantic salmon swims _____ kilometres in the ocean every year.
10. The green turtle travels _____ kilometres from South America to Ascension Island.
11. The elk roams _____ kilometres around northern Canada every year.
12. The albatross flies _____ kilometres across the world, from west to east.

Hibernation

Use these words to complete the paragraph.

climates   sleep   animals   turtles   winter

Many animals hibernate in the _____. This means that they have a long, deep
      1
_____. They sleep in a cave or under the ground. Animals that live in cold
2
_____ do this to escape the cold. Some _____ that hibernate are frogs, toads,
3   **4**
lizards, mice, bats, bears, snails, _____, hedgehogs and squirrels.
                                    5

The Four Seasons: Spring

> **Video Activity 2: Part 1**

Exercise 1: Discuss

Discuss these questions in a group.

1. How many seasons are there in Canada?
2. What are the approximate dates of each season?
3. What happens to the snow and ice in the spring?
4. Where are the animals in the winter when there is snow and ice everywhere?

Exercise 2: Predict

Discuss these statements in a group. Answer true or false. If the statement is false, correct the information.

1. Floods are common in the spring.
2. The days get longer in the spring.
3. Baby animals are born in the spring.
4. All birds' eggs are white.
5. The weather is very hot in the spring.

| **Did You Know?** | Animals know when to hibernate by the change in temperature. For example, the hedgehog goes to sleep when the temperature falls. The hedgehog's body temperature falls, and stays low while it sleeps. |

Exercise 3: Get Ready to Watch the Video

☐☐ Read the questions aloud with a partner .

1. What are some things that change with the seasons?
2. In spring, the days get _____ and _____.
3. What is migration?
4. What do Canada geese do when they land in the field?
5. What bird appears to tell you that spring is coming?
6. In spring, the snow melts. Name two places it goes.
7. Why do floods sometimes happen in spring?
8. What is the snow fence used for?
9. As the days lengthen, the earth _____ and becomes _____.
10. What do farmers do to their fields in the spring?
11. Which plant is called the pussy willow?

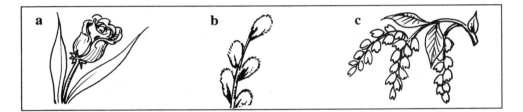

12. Why do Canada geese return to the pond on the farm?
13. Which of the following do we find in or around the pond?

   a) the leopard frog   f) frogs' eggs
   b) dogs   g) deer
   c) insect larvae   h) snails
   d) tadpoles   i) the woodchuck
   e) geese   j) goats

14. Name these things.

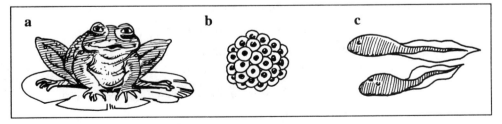

15. Male birds sing to attract mates.   **T** (true) or **F** (false)?
16. What is a cardinal, and what colour is it?
17. Describe the beaver.
18. What is it doing?

Exercise 4: Watch the Video for General Ideas

Watch the video. What are some topics that are discussed?

Exercise 5: Watch the Video for Details

Go back to the questions in Exercise 3. While you watch the video, answer the questions.

The Four Seasons: Spring

Video Activity 2: Part 2

Exercise 1: Discuss

Discuss these questions in a group.

1. Name some changes we see in the spring.
2. What happens when the snow melts?
3. What does the farmer do in the spring?
4. What kind of life is there around and in the pond?

Exercise 2: Get Ready to Watch the Video

Read the questions aloud with a partner .

1. Many animals are born in the spring.   **T** (true) or **F** (false)?
2. Match the word with its definition.

    a buck   a female deer

    a doe   a baby deer

    a fawn   a male deer

3. What colour are robins' eggs?
4. Complete the chart on the worksheet.

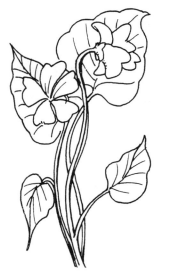

Name of flower	Colour of flower
marsh marigold	
violet	
trillium	

5. What colour is the robin?
6. Young birds don't eat much. **T F**
7. What does the squirrel do in winter?
8. What are lambs?
9. What is the farmer planting?
10. The farmer's plants need _____ and _____ to grow tall.
11. What are blossoms?
12. Apples are picked in _____.
13. Canada geese fly _____ in autumn.
14. What happens to some tadpoles?
15. The sun is _____ and the sky is _____.
16. Leaves help us because they _____.
17. Leaves help birds because they _____.
18. Baby robins eat _____ and _____.
19. What is camouflage?
20. Why is camouflage useful?
21. What will the farmer do with his corn?
22. The days get shorter in spring. **T F**
23. What must the baby ducks learn?
24. List the changes that come with the end of spring.

 ## Exercise 3: Watch the Video for General Ideas

Watch the video. What are some topics that are discussed?

 ## Exercise 4: Watch the Video for Details

Go back to the questions in Exercise 2. While you watch, answer the questions.

What About You?

Exercise 1: Get Ready

Discuss these questions in a group.

Describe two seasons in another country or region that you know about. Here are some things to talk about:

1. temperatures
2. length of day
3. weather conditions (rain, snow, etc.)
4. changes to trees and plants
5. types of clothing worn
6. kinds of food grown
7. people's reactions to the weather

Exercise 2: Write

Write about two seasons in Canada, or in another country that you know about. Use the information from the previous exercise.

The North: Climate and Weather

Canada – Hot and Cold

Exercise 1: Get Ready

What do you know about the climate in Canada? Work in a group. Choose the best answer.

When you have finished, turn to page 86 to check your answers.

1. Which Canadian city has the mildest climate?

    a) Charlottetown, PEI

    b) Victoria, BC

    c) Quebec City, Quebec

2. Which is the windiest place on earth?

    a) the Canadian Arctic

    b) Antarctica

    c) the Himalayas

3. What is the coldest temperature ever recorded in the northern hemisphere?

    a) −48° Celsius

    b) −78° Celsius

    c) −68° Celsius

4. What is the highest temperature ever recorded in Canada?

    a) 38° Celsius

    b) 42° Celsius

    c) 45° Celsius

5. The coldest capital city in the world is:

    a) Ottawa, Canada

    b) Oslo, Norway

    c) Ulaanbaatar, Mongolia

6. Which city has the highest average temperature?

    a) New York, USA

    b) Reykjavik, Iceland

    c) Toronto, Canada

7. Which of these is the most dangerous natural phenomenon for Canadians?

    a) avalanches

    b) lightning

    c) cold weather

8. How big were the biggest hail pellets ever seen in Canada?

    a) the size of green peas

    b) the size of golf balls

    c) the size of tennis balls

9. Which insects fell from the sky when it rained in Red Creek, BC on October 14, 1934?

    a) beetles

    b) butterflies

    c) grasshoppers

10. Why did July 11 become a special weather day in Canada?

    a) it had the hottest temperatures

    b) it had the wettest weather

    c) it had the most surprises

Life in the Arctic

Exercise 1: Get Ready to Read

What do you know about the Arctic? Discuss these questions in a group.
Answer **T** (true) or **F** (false).

1. Western Canada is part of the Arctic.
2. It is so cold in the Arctic that no plants or animals can live there.
3. Traditionally, the Inuit made houses out of snow.
4. In the summer, the Arctic weather is hot.
5. There are mountains and forests in the Arctic.
6. Flowers can grow in the Arctic climate.
7. The Inuit get food from farming and from hunting.
8. Life for the Inuit has not changed much in the last century.

Exercise 2: Read Quickly to Increase Speed

Work with a partner. Read one paragraph at a time. After each paragraph, stop and answer the questions.

Life in the Arctic

A. One of the last great wilderness regions on earth is the area known as the Arctic. The Arctic is a region of 72.5 million square kilometres. It includes the northern parts of Canada, Alaska and parts of Europe and Asia. About 50 000 Inuit live in northern Canada, Alaska and Greenland today. The Inuit live with the ice and snow of the Arctic. They have 28 words to describe different kinds of snow. These words tell them if the snow is hard enough to travel over or soft enough to bury a trap. The Inuit need this information because they go off for weeks at a time to hunt. When hunters travelled away from their villages in the past, they even used the snow to build houses called igloos to protect them from the cold.

B. The Arctic has a harsh climate. In winter the days are very short and very dark. The temperature can fall to −50° Celsius. The land is full of ice and snow. In summer the days are very long. The sun never really sets in the summer. It is light 24 hours a day. The average temperature is 10° Celsius. It never gets very hot and sometimes it snows in the summer. The Inuit divide the year into six seasons to show the changes that take place during the year. The Arctic is cold and icy, but it is not empty or barren. The Arctic region has great mountain ranges, the largest forests in the world and many interesting animals and plants. Even in the high Arctic, above the tree line, there is a rich population of sea and land animals. There is also a rich display of summer plants and flowers.

C. In traditional Inuit culture people survived the cold climate because they knew how to keep warm. In winter they wore fur clothing and slept on fur blankets. They got the fur from animals that they killed. They wore two layers of fur. The layer near their skin had the fur turned to the inside. The second layer had the fur turned to the outside. On their feet they wore fur boots called mukluks. The bottoms were made of moose or seal skin. The tops were made of caribou skin. Some Inuit still keep these traditions alive. Traditionally, the Inuit were a nomadic people. They moved from place to place to look for food. Now, Inuit customs and traditions are mixing with modern ways. Modern houses, weapons and transportation are bringing changes to the Arctic.

Paragraph A

1. Where is the Arctic?
2. How many Inuit live in Canada, Alaska and Greenland today?
3. How many words do the Inuit have for snow?
4. What is hard snow good for?
5. What is soft snow good for?
6. When did the Inuit hunters build igloos?

Paragraph B

7. Describe winter days in the Arctic.
8. How low can the temperature fall in the winter?
9. How many hours of daylight are there in the summer?
10. What is the average temperature in summer?
11. How many seasons do the Inuit count?
12. What kind of plant and animal life is there in the Arctic?

Paragraph C

13. Name two things the Inuit made from fur.
14. How many layers does fur clothing have?
15. Describe the layers.
16. Describe the fur boots that the Inuit wore.
17. Name some things that are changing in the Inuit lifestyle.

Exercise 3: Read Carefully for Details

Read the text again. Write the answers to the questions.

Exercise 4: Review Ideas

Work with a partner. Match these facts.

Cause:	Effect:
The sun never really sets.	They have 28 words for snow.
They want to show changes in the climate.	They build snow houses.
They need information about snow conditions.	They survived.
They need protection from the cold on hunting trips.	They divide the year into six seasons.
They knew how to keep warm.	It is light 24 hours a day.
They needed to find food.	They moved from place to place.

Exercise 5: Practise Writing

Write the sentences that you matched. Use **so** to show the result, or effect.

Example: The sun never really sets **so** it is light 24 hours a day.

Silent Letters

Write these words. Cross out the letters that are not pronounced.

Example: Ar∅tic

listen	often	island
answer	half	calm
knife	write	know
knee	comb	lamb

The Walrus

> **Listening Activity 9**

Exercise 1: Get Ready to Listen

The walrus lives in the Arctic. It lives on the ice near the ocean.

☐ ☐   Look at the picture of the walrus. With a partner, predict the answers to the questions.

1. The walrus weighs:
    a) 90 kilograms
    b) 450 kilograms
    c) 900 kilograms

2. Most of the time the walrus eats:
    a) algae
    b) fish
    c) shellfish

3. The walrus's two white tusks are used for:
    a) protection
    b) hunting
    c) digging clams

4. The Inuit use the walrus:
    a) as food
    b) as pets
    c) as shelter

5. Walruses live:
    a) alone
    b) on the ice
    c) in colonies

 Exercise 2: Listen for Meaning

Listen to the story to understand the general idea.

 Exercise 3: Listen for Details

Read these questions aloud with a partner. Then listen and answer the questions.

1. Say three things that describe the walrus.
2. How much does the walrus weigh?
3. What does the walrus eat?
4. Name two things the walrus uses its tusks for.
5. How deep can the walrus dive?
6. How long can the walrus stay under water?
7. How do the Inuit use the following parts of the walrus?

   a) meat 　　　　　　d) skin

   b) muscles 　　　　　e) whiskers

   c) tusks

8. How many walruses live in a colony?
9. Who are the walrus's enemies?
10. Explain how walruses protect each other.

Exercise 4: Tell the Story

Tell the story of the walrus to your partner. Use your own words. Then your partner will tell you the story.

Exercise 5: Write the Story

Write everything that you remember about the walrus.

Canada – Hot and Cold: Answers

Exercise 2: Read For Information

Read the information. Check your answers from page 80.

1. St. John's, Newfoundland has the worst climate (the most extreme). Victoria, BC has the mildest climate in Canada (not too hot, not too cold).

2. The windiest place on earth is not in the Arctic. It is Antarctica, which holds a record of 122 days of strong winds.

3. The coldest temperature recorded in the northern hemisphere was in Siberia, where the temperature fell to −68° Celsius.

4. The highest temperature recorded in Canada was in Midale and Yellow Grass, Saskatchewan. The temperature soared to 45° Celsius.

5. The coldest capital in the world isn't Ottawa (it just feels that way). It is Ulaanbaatar, which is the capital of Mongolia. Ottawa is the second coldest capital city in the world.

6. Reykjavik, the capital of Iceland, is just below the Arctic Circle. Surprisingly, it has a higher average temperature than the city of New York, which is further south than Paris, France!

7. Extreme cold is three times more dangerous to people in Canada than lightning and avalanches combined.

8. In 1984, near Brandon, Manitoba, hail the size of golf balls fell from the sky. It killed a lot of crops, but fortunately no people. This was much better than in southwest China, where dog-sized hailstones killed and injured many people.

Did You Know? "Freeze-up" takes place in the north in October or November. This is when lakes and rivers freeze for the winter. Freeze-up makes it easier for the Inuit to travel in winter than in summer.

9. In 1934, at Red Creek, BC, beetles fell from the sky when it rained. Probably they were swept up by strong winds and came down with the rain.

10. In the history of Canadian weather two days are special. October 2 is special because it has had no surprises. It is the most unexciting weather day of the year. July 11 is called Canadian Weather Day. More surprising weather events have happened on this day than on any other. July 11 has had floods, tornadoes, storms and mud slides.

Sports and Recreation

About Sports

Exercise 1: Get Ready

Work in a group. Look at the pictures of different sports. Name the sports you see in the pictures.

Exercise 2: Match

Write the names of the sports where you:

1. play on ice
2. play on a field
3. play in summer
4. play in winter
5. play in a team
6. play alone
7. use a ball
8. use a net
9. wear a helmet
10. wear a uniform
11. wear a bathing suit
12. use a stick
13. wear skates
14. play in a gymnasium

Unusual Sports

Choose the correct word for each space.

tennis   wrestler   team   people   country   sports

Some sports are international. For example, most _____ know about football,
                                                    1

_____ and golf. They may even have played one of these games or watched
2

them on TV. Other sports are special to one _____ or region. Sumo
                                            3

wrestling, ski-jumping, cricket and baseball are not international _____.
                                                                  4

Can you imagine a Norwegian sumo _____, a French baseball player or a
                                 5

Mexican ski-jumper? Can you imagine a Russian cricket _____?
                                                      6

What About You?

Discuss these questions in a group.

1. Match the national sport and the country.

    Spain   cricket
    Japan   soccer
    Canada   bull-fighting
    England   baseball
    Brazil   judo
    the United States   hockey

2. What sports are popular in your culture?

3. Describe a sport that you like to play or watch. Give information about:

    a) where you play
    b) the equipment you need
    c) the rules of the game

Did You Know?   In the summer in Canada, sports you would expect to see in the parks
include soccer, football and baseball. Running and biking are also popular.
In the winter, skiing and skating are popular. People don't skate on outdoor
rinks as much as they used to, however. Skating and hockey frequently take
place at indoor rinks.

Roller-skating

Choose the correct word for each space.

wheels   places   skates   activity   paths   parking

Roller-skating is a very popular _____ these days. People go to special
                                   1

_____ called roller rinks to roller-skate for exercise and fun. You can often
2

see people speeding along _____ in the park or even along city streets.
                            3

Teenagers with blade _____ play hockey in alleys and _____ lots. Roller-
                       4   **5**

skating is safe and easy today. Roller-skates have specially designed _____
                                                                         6

that make them easy to control. It is easy to turn and easy to stop .

A Grand Entrance

Exercise 1: Get Ready to Read

Work in a group. Discuss these questions.

1. Did you ever roller-skate?
2. Was it easy?
3. How have roller-skates changed from the past?

Exercise 2: Read and Recall

Read the text quickly. Then work with a partner to see how many questions
you can answer from memory.

A Grand Entrance

Before 1750 the idea of skating on wheels didn't exist. In that year a man
named Joseph Merlin was living in Belgium. Merlin's work was
manufacturing musical instruments. In his spare time he liked to play the
violin. Joseph Merlin was a man with many ideas and many dreams. People
called him a dreamer.

One day Merlin received an invitation to attend a costume party. He was very
pleased and a little excited. As the day of the party came near Merlin began to
make plans. He wanted to find a way to make a grand entrance at the party.
Merlin had an idea. He thought that he would attract a lot of attention if he

could put wheels under his shoes. His plan was to attach the wheels to his shoes so that he could roll into the party and surprise everyone.

Merlin tried different things to make himself roll into a room. Finally, he decided to attach two wheels to each shoe. These were the first roller skates. Merlin was very proud of his invention. He dreamed of arriving at the party and rolling into the room playing the violin. He was sure that everyone would be amazed.

The night of the party Merlin rolled into the room playing his violin. Everyone was astonished to see him. There was just one problem. Merlin had no way to stop his roller skates. He rolled on playing the violin. Then, with all eyes on him, Merlin crashed into a huge mirror that was hanging on the wall. The mirror broke into many pieces with a very loud noise. Nobody forgot Merlin's grand entrance for a long time.

1. Where did the story take place?
2. What was Merlin's job?
3. What instrument did he play?
4. What kind of party was he invited to attend?
5. What was Merlin's plan?
6. Describe Merlin's roller skates.
7. How did people react to Merlin's grand entrance?
8. What went wrong?

Exercise 3: Read Carefully for Details

Work with a partner. Go back to Exercise 2. Read carefully and check your answers.

Exercise 4: Tell the Story

Tell the story of the grand entrance to your partner. Use your own words. Then your partner will tell you the story.

Exercise 5: Write the Story

Write the story of the grand entrance.

Lacrosse

Listening Activity 10

Exercise 1: Get Ready to Listen

☐ ☐ Read the questions aloud with a partner. What do you think the story will be about?

1. Where did lacrosse originate?

2. Baggattaway was the original name for the game we call lacrosse. **T** (true) or **F** (false)?

3. How long did the game last?

4. How many teams played?

5. Only local teams played the game.   **T F**

6. How many players were on the team?

7. What injuries did players sometimes have?

8. Give two reasons that baggattaway was important to the Native peoples.

9. Name two pieces of equipment that were used to play baggattaway.

10. Why did the settlers call the game lacrosse?

11. Lacrosse was the most popular game in Canada by 1850.   **T F**

12. Name two provinces where lacrosse is played today.

13. Name two places where players go to play lacrosse today.

Exercise 2: Listen for Meaning

Listen to the story. What is the story about?

Exercise 3: Listen for Details

Go back to the questions in Exercise 1. While you listen, answer the questions.

Exercise 4: Tell the Story

Tell the story of lacrosse to a partner. Use your own words. Then your partner will tell you the story.

Exercise 5: Write the Story

Write everything that you remember about the story of lacrosse.

The Y

Exercise 1: Get Ready to Read

Discuss these questions in a group.

1. What do the letters YMCA and YWCA stand for?
2. Who can join the Y?
3. What are some things you can do at the Y?

Exercise 2: Read Quickly for General Ideas

The Y

Who in North America doesn't know about the Y? This name was short for the YMCA, which stands for Young Men's Christian Association. But that really doesn't tell the story today. The **Y** isn't only for young people. It has residences, community activities and sports programmes for people of all ages. The **M** isn't only for men. There is the YWCA with residences and sports programmes for women. The **C** isn't only for Christian. The Y has members from every race and religion. It is non-denominational. There is

even the YMHA/YWHA (where the **H** stands for Hebrew). The **A** isn't only for association. It is for swimming pools, summer camps, leadership programmes and adult education.

The YMCA began in London, England in 1844. The founder was a man named George Williams. There is a university in Montreal named after Sir George Williams. It is part of Concordia University today. The YWCA began in 1855 in London. Both organizations are very successful. Members come from many different backgrounds.

The Y is probably best known for its residences. They are clean, safe, friendly and cheap. You can find them in nearly every city in Canada and the United States.

The Y is also well known for its sports programmes. The Y owns millions of dollars' worth of property. Its buildings have good sports facilities such as gyms and swimming pools. There are many different sports programmes where people can learn everything from swimming to self defence.

People go to the Y after school or after work to lift weights, do aerobics, swim, play basketball or maybe go jogging on the roof of the building.

Some of the most popular summer camps belong to the Y too. Children from rich and poor families go to camps in the country. At camp they can swim, go canoeing and learn about nature. Many campers have good memories of sitting around the campfire singing and making new friends through the Y.

The Y now has a large variety of educational courses. Experienced teachers provide courses in everything from computers to career counselling. You can even learn how to fill in your tax returns at the Y.

Today, the local Y is an important part of many communities, where people can acquire new skills, take courses that are not very expensive, and meet their neighbours while they get fit. It offers programmes for everyone, from day-care services for young children to clubs for seniors. Family members can go for a swim together, learn to speak a new language, learn how to repair a car, or take a course to practise speaking in public. Over the years the Y has continued to change. It provides many new services for our changing world.

Exercise 3: Read Carefully for Details

Work with a partner. Look in the text for the answers.

1. What do the letters YMCA stand for?
2. What age group does the Y serve?
3. What are some services that the YWCA provides?
4. What religion are members of the YMCA? The YMHA?
5. What are some things the Y offers?
6. Where and when did the YMCA begin? The YWCA?
7. Give five facts about the residences.
8. What kind of sports facilities can you find at the Y?
9. What are some sports activities that people like to do at the Y?
10. Who goes to summer camp?
11. What are some camp activities?
12. Describe some educational courses at the Y.
13. Give three ways that the Y is an important part of the community.
14. Who does the Y provide services for? Give examples.
15. Is the Y the same as it was in the past? Explain.

Exercise 4: Practise Numbers

Write the numbers that your teacher dictates.

1. The YMCA has about _____ members, in more than 90 different countries.
2. In Canada, more than _____ people take part in programmes at the YMCA.
3. In the United States, about _____ people take part in activities at the YMCA.
4. The YWCA has over _____ members in 80 different countries.
5. The YWCA employees about _____ people.
6. There are about _____ volunteers at the YWCA.
7. In the United States, the YWCA has programmes in more than _____ locations.
8. In total, the YMCA has about _____ gymnasiums and pools.
9. The YMCA also operates about _____ health and fitness centres.
10. There are about _____ courts for tennis and other ball games at the YMCA.

Saying Numbers: Millions

Partner A

Cover Partner B's section.

Read these numbers to your partner. Then write the numbers that your partner reads to you. Use the worksheet.

96 000 000	_____
63 000 000	_____
278 000 000	_____
719 000 000	_____
304 000 000	_____

Now change roles. Write the numbers that your partner reads to you. Then read these numbers to your partner.

_____	23 486 000
_____	97 622 000
_____	418 666 000
_____	902 759 000
_____	92 421 000

Partner B

Cover Partner A's section.

Write the numbers that your partner reads to you. Then read these numbers to your partner. Use the worksheet.

_____	84 000 000
_____	36 000 000
_____	319 000 000
_____	917 000 000
_____	403 000 000

Now change roles. Read these numbers to your partner. Then write the numbers that your partner reads to you.

28 626 000	_____
88 268 000	_____
519 339 000	_____
407 691 000	_____
47 324 000	_____

Joining the Y

Listening Activity 11

Exercise 1: Get Ready to Listen

☐☐ Read the questions aloud with a partner. What do you think the conversation will be about?

1.   What does the man want information about?
2.   Who had the idea for the man to join an exercise programme?
3.   What days are the men's aerobics classes?
4.   What time is the men's aerobics class?
5.   How often is the mixed class?
6.   What questions does the man ask about the jogging track?
7.   Who can use the weight-lifting equipment?
8.   How can the man become a member of the Y?
9.   Who needs a doctor's certificate?
10. What is the man interested in?

🔘🔘 Exercise 2: Listen for Meaning

Listen to the conversation. What is the conversation about?

🔘🔘 Exercise 3: Listen for Details

Go back to the questions in Exercise 1. While you listen, answer the questions.

Unit 11

The Environment

Packaging

Choose the correct word for each space.

fruit   jars   people   plastic   metal

North Americans consume 30 times more of the earth's resources than _____
                                                                        1

in other societies. Think about packaging, for example. In the supermarket,

meat, _____ and vegetables have cardboard or styrofoam under them, and
      2

_____ over them. Many of the things that we eat and drink are in packages.
3

Jam comes in glass _____ ; juice comes in plastic bottles; soup comes in
                   4

_____ cans. Packaging is everywhere.
5

The Garbage Quiz

Exercise 1: Get Ready

What do you know about the garbage we throw away every day? Do this quiz and find out. Discuss the questions in a group.

When you have finished, turn to page 108. Read the information to check your answers.

1. Which of these things makes up most of our garbage?

   a) glass

   b) metal

   c) paper

2. What happens to most of the garbage that is collected?

   a) It is burned in incinerators.

   b) It is dumped in a hole in the ground.

   c) It is buried in the ground.

3. What is the problem with garbage dumps?

   a) They smell bad.

   b) They look bad.

   c) They use too much land.

4. Why is it bad to burn garbage?

   a) It becomes too hot.

   b) It puts harmful chemicals into the air.

   c) It has an unpleasant smell.

5. The amount of styrofoam thrown out each day in North America can make:

   a) 5 thousand coffee cups

   b) 17 million coffee cups

   c) 900 million coffee cups

6. Which items do you think North Americans throw away the most each year? Put these in order:

   a) plastic razors

   b) car tires

   c) pens

7. If you throw a glass bottle away in a forest, how long will it last?

   a) a hundred years

   b) a year and a half

   c) a thousand years

8. How is most aluminum used?

   a) to make drink containers

   b) to make doors and windows

   c) to make airplanes

9. If you recycle one aluminum can, the energy saved can:

   a) be used to make a new can

   b) operate a television set for three hours

   c) operate a hair dryer for an hour

10. The newsprint used to make newspapers in Canada **each day** comes from how many trees?

    a) 4000 trees

    b) 40 000 trees

    c) 400 000 trees

11. What is half the plastic we throw away each year used for?

    a) packaging

    b) shampoo bottles

    c) razors

12. When you spend $10.00 on food, how much money is for the packing?

    a) $0.50

    b) $1.00

    c) $1.50

Too Much Garbage

Exercise 1: Get Ready to Read

Discuss these questions in a group.

1. Which foods usually come in packages?

2. What are some different kinds of packages that you see in the supermarket?

3. Which foods can you buy loose (not in packages)?

4. Which kinds of packages are easy to recycle? Which are not?

5. What can you do if you see products in packages that cannot be recycled?

Exercise 2: Read Quickly for General Ideas

Too Much Garbage

What do eating a chocolate bar, using a new plastic razor and buying a man's shirt have in common? All of these things are wrapped in layers of packaging. All of this packaging goes into the garbage.

If we dumped the average Canadian's garbage from the last year onto a doorstep, this is what we would find: The garbage would fill up the living-room, the kitchen, most of the bedroom and part of the bathroom. There would be plastic bags, food scraps, old newspapers, junk mail, broken glass, boxes, cleaners, batteries, medicines, diapers and many other things.

What happens to your garbage when you put it outside your door to be collected? Usually the garbage goes to a landfill site. A landfill site is a field with a big hole where we dump our garbage. When we keep adding more garbage to it, it becomes a mountain — a mountain of garbage.

Canada is a nation of consumers. This means that we buy a lot of products. Most of the products we buy are wrapped in paper, styrofoam and plastic. After we buy the products, we throw out the paper and plastic. We also throw away many products after we use them once or twice. The average Canadian household produces 1 tonne of garbage every year. In total, Canadians produce 27 million tonnes of garbage every year.

Now we have a problem: What can we do with all this garbage? Many landfill sites are closing because they are full. We will soon have no more place to put our garbage.

Another problem is that all the garbage we produce is a waste of natural resources. Thousands of trees are cut down every day to make paper products and newspapers. Oil is used to make millions of plastic bags and food containers each week. Thousands of tonnes of steel are used each day to make cans for food and drinks.

A third problem is that we use energy to produce all of these products. This energy could be used for more important things, such as heating our homes.

A fourth problem is that when products are manufactured, chemicals are used. These chemicals often go into the air as smoke during the manufacturing process. They pollute the air that we breathe. Also, when manufacturers are finished with the chemicals, they often dump them into rivers or oceans, or bury them in the ground, where they can get into our drinking water.

Fortunately, there are things we can do to reduce our garbage. We can avoid excess packaging by choosing the products that have the least amount of packaging. We can use things more than one time. We can recycle many things to make new products.

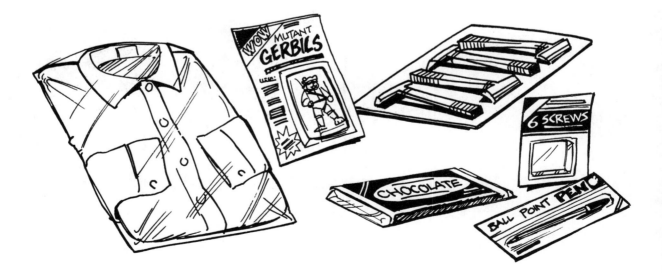

Exercise 3: Read Carefully for Details

Work with a partner. Look in the text for the answers.

1. What happens to extra packaging?
2. Name some things that are in the average person's garbage.
3. What is a landfill site?
4. What is a consumer?
5. How are most of the products that we buy wrapped?
6. How much garbage is produced each year in Canada:
   a) by the average household?
   b) in total?
7. Why can't we continue to put garbage into landfill sites?
8. Which natural resources do we use to produce these products?
   a) paper products
   b) plastic bags
   c) newspapers
   d) cans for food
9. What is a better way to use our energy supply?
10. How do chemicals from manufacturing get into the air? How are they harmful?
11. How do chemicals get into our water? How are they harmful?
12. List three ways we can reduce our garbage.

The Three R's

If you want to help reduce garbage, you can follow the three R's of the environmental movement: reduce, reuse, recycle.

 ## Exercise 1: Read Carefully for Information

Read each paragraph, then choose the word that matches the description.

reduce   reuse   recycle

A. You can write on both sides of a piece of paper. When you buy food that comes in a plastic container, you can save the container and use it again later to keep other food fresh. You can give clothes that you don't wear any more to other people. You can use many things more than once.

B. If you change your buying habits, you will not have so much garbage in the first place. Try not to buy disposable items such as plastic razors or paper cups. Try to buy products that do not have a lot of packaging.

C. Many things can be used again in a different way. For example, glass bottles can be melted and made into new bottles. Plastic from food containers is being made into park benches. Newspaper can be used to make cardboard and other paper products.

Exercise 2: Recall Information

Work with a partner. Close your book. How many suggestions can you remember? Make a list.

Exercise 3: Express Yourself

In a group, discuss ways that you can reduce, recycle and reuse things that you buy. Add your ideas to the list.

Recycling

In the supermarket, there are many different kinds of foods. Most of these foods come in some kind of package. Foods come in boxes, cans, jars and bottles. Some kinds of packages are easy to recycle. Other kinds cannot be recycled.

Packages and Containers

Listening Activity 12

Exercise 1: Get Ready to Listen

Look at the pictures of food in containers. Work in a group and discuss these questions.

1. What is each container made of?
2. Do you think that each container can be recycled? Can it be reused?

Did You Know?   Look for this symbol on products that you buy. It is the recycling symbol. It shows that an item can be recycled. The three arrows are for the different things that can be recycled: solids, liquids and gases.

Exercise 2: Listen for Details

While you listen, check (✔) the kind of package that is used. Some things come in more than one container. Check all the containers. Use the worksheet.

	Cardboard/Paper	Plastic	Glass	Aluminum	Styrofoam
soup					
soft drinks					
meat					
rice					
mayonnaise					
orange juice					
juice box					
cookies					
eggs					
a pen					
tuna					
ketchup					
milk					

Did You Know?   Many cities in Canada have a "blue box" programme for recycling garbage. People are encouraged to separate their garbage and put things that can be recycled into the blue boxes. These blue boxes are picked up once a week and taken to recycling centres. Then paper, glass and plastics are made into new products.

Exercise 3: Listen Again for Details

While you listen to a description of each package, circle the items that you can recycle.

The Garbage Quiz: Answers

Exercise 2: Read for Information

Read the information. Check your answers to the quiz on pages 101-102.

1. About one third of all the garbage we throw out is made of paper. Another third comes from food scraps. The final third is a mixture of glass, metal, plastic and wood.

2. Most of the garbage that is collected is dumped in a hole in the ground called a landfill site.

3. Landfill sites are filling up quickly. In many cities, landfill sites are closing because there is no more room for garbage. City and provincial governments have to find new ways to deal with our garbage.

4. Burning garbage releases chemicals into the air. Many of these chemicals are harmful to our health.

5. Styrofoam, a kind of plastic, is used to make fast-food containers, take-out coffee cups and many other things. Every day, thousands of tonnes of styrofoam are thrown out. If we used all the styrofoam that people in North America threw out in one day, we could make 900 million styrofoam coffee cups!

6. Every year North Americans throw away over 16 billion disposable diapers, one and a half billion plastic pens, over two billion plastic razors and 220 million car tires.

7. If you throw away a glass bottle in a forest, it will last a long time. It will still be there for your great-grandchildren to see. In fact, it will last for about a thousand years.

8. Aluminum is used to make airplanes, cars, household items and many other things. The largest use of aluminum is for cans for drinks such as cola and beer.

9. It is much more expensive to make a new can from metal than to recycle a can. The energy saved from recycling one can would be enough to power your television set for three hours.

10. The number of trees that are cut down every day to make paper for Canada's newspapers is over 40 000 trees. This is the number of trees in many forests!

11. We use plastic for many things, from combs to pens to razors. However, half of all the plastic we use is in the form of packaging, including plastic bags from supermarkets and other stores.

12. When you spend $10 on food, about one dollar is spent on the packaging and bags you use to take the food home. This packaging is thrown away as soon as you get home.

Did You Know?	In Canada, getting rid of garbage is the responsibility of provincial governments. For example, in Prince Edward Island, the government does not allow stores to sell non-refillable soft-drink bottles. In Manitoba, there is a tax on alcoholic drink containers that are non-refillable.

North America

The North America Quiz

Work in a group. Use the maps on page x and page 112 to help you answer the questions.

1. The continent of North America is:

   a) the largest continent in the world

   b) the second largest continent in the world

   c) the third largest continent in the world

2. Which country has the greatest land size?

   a) Canada

   b) the United States

   c) Mexico

3. Which country has the biggest population?

   a) Canada

   b) the United States

   c) Mexico

4. The largest freshwater lake in North America is:

   a) Lake Louise

   b) Lake Michigan

   c) Lake Superior

5. Which country in North America has the longest coastline?

   a) Canada

   b) the United States

   c) Mexico

6. Which country has the most lakes and rivers?

   a) Canada

   b) the United States

   c) Mexico

7. Which city has the largest population?

   a) Toronto

   b) New York

   c) Mexico City

8. The number of major languages used in North America is:

   a) two

   b) three

   c) four

9. Which river runs between Canada and the United States?

   a) the Mississippi

   b) the Rio Grande

   c) the St. Lawrence

10. Which river runs between the United States and Mexico?

   a) the St. Lawrence

   b) the Rio Grande

   c) the Columbia

Did You Know?   Northern Canada lies within the Arctic Circle. In summer, the sun shines for 24 hours a day. In winter, it is dark 24 hours a day.

North America, Then and Now

📖 **Exercise 1: Read Quickly for General Ideas**

North America, Then and Now

Four hundred years ago North America had no countries. It was one large continent that extended from the Arctic Ocean in the north to the Caribbean Sea in the south. In those days, before we had airplanes and ships that could cross the oceans, the continent of North America, like South America, was isolated from the rest of the world by the Atlantic and the Pacific Oceans.

5 The population of the Americas was very big at that time. Agriculture became important in Mexico in 2000 BC and in other parts of North America in the 1500 years that followed. Population grew as a result of a sure supply of food. In 300 AD the southern Mexican city of Teotechuacan had a population of a quarter of a million people. It was bigger than London, England and was probably the biggest city in the world.

10 When European explorers first came to America after 1492, there were one million members of Inuit and Indians nations in the region of Canada. There were between five and ten million Native people in the area of the United States. There were probably between forty and seventy million Native people in
15 the area of Mexico, Central and South America. Tragically, diseases that were brought by the European explorers and settlers in the sixteenth century killed 90 percent of the Native people.

Today North America is divided into three countries: Canada,
20 the United States and Mexico. Canada and the United States are separated by the 49th parallel of latitude. This is the longest undefended border in the world. It crosses forests, farmland, prairies and mountains between the Atlantic and Pacific coasts. The border of the United States and Mexico runs between the
25 Pacific Ocean and the Gulf of Mexico along the Rio Grande River.

Canada is a big country with a small population. It covers an enormous land area but has a population of only twenty-seven million. Many Canadians live in cities such as Montreal, Toronto or Vancouver or in towns across the southern part of the country. Canada's population includes immigrants who
30 have come from many parts of the world. Different groups of people in Canada communicate with each other in English or French.

The United States has a population of two hundred million people and it covers a very big land area (although it is smaller than Canada in size). Americans have also come from many different parts of the world. The United States has many very big cities with important industries and commercial
35 activities. It has famous universities and cultural attractions such the Statue of Liberty and Disneyland.

Mexico is a smaller country than Canada or the United States. Many Mexicans live in small towns or villages. At the same time Mexico City, which is the capital, is an important centre for industry, government and culture. It also has a huge population that makes it the largest city in the world. The
40 language of communication is Spanish.

Exercise 2: Read Carefully for Details

Work with a partner. Look in the text for the answers.

1. Why were the Americas isolated until 400 years ago?
2. Where did agriculture become very important?
3. What change did agriculture bring?
4. What was Teotechuacan? Give details.
5. Make a chart similar to the one below. Complete the information.

Region	Population
Canada	
	40 – 70 million

6. What tragedy happened in the sixteenth century?
7. What is the 49th parallel?
8. In what parts of Canada do many Canadians live?
9. Where do Americans come from?
10. Name two cultural attractions in the United States.
11. Which is the smallest country in North America?
12. What is special about the capital of Mexico?

Exercise 3: Contextual Reference

Give the reference for the words in bold type.

1. In line 2, **in those days** refers to:
2. In line 5, **at that time** refers to:
3. In line 8, **it** refers to:
4. In line 21, **this** refers to:
5. In line 22, **it** refers to:
6. In line 27, **it** refers to:
7. In line 32, **it** refers to:
8. In line 35, **it** refers to:
9. In line 39, **it** refers to:

Exercise 4: Review Vocabulary

☐☐ Match similar words or expressions.

ocean	separated
enormous	boundary
region	sea
Inuit and Indian nations	covers
divided	area
border	city
town	farming
agriculture	Native peoples
population	huge
extends	people

Families of the World: Mexico

Video Activity 3: Part 1

Exercise 1: Get Ready to Watch the Video

MEXICO CITY

☐☐ Read the questions aloud with a partner.

1. Puebla is the _____ largest city in Mexico.
2. How many people live in Puebla?
3. Puebla is both a traditional and a modern city. **T** (true) or **F** (false)?
4. Alejandra is _____ years old.
5. The ages of the other children in Alejandra's family are _____, _____ and _____.
6. Which three countries is Mexico near?
7. What body of water is to the west of Mexico?
8. What is the capital of Mexico?
9. Why does Alejandra want to learn English?
10. What job does Alejandra's father have?
11. What is special about Friday in the Prado family?
12. When is the main meal of the day?
    a) morning   b) early afternoon   c) evening
13. In Mexico, a family of four is considered:
    a) small   b) average   c) large

14. Why does the family like to buy its tamales ready made?

15. What are some chores the family members do on Saturday?

16. Why is Mrs. Prado good at running the family?

17. Why do the Prados need a water pump?

18. What does the mother buy in the supermarket?

19. The mother buys tortillas in the supermarket.   **T   F**

Exercise 2: Watch the Video for General Ideas

Watch the video. What are some topics that are discussed?

Exercise 3: Watch the Video for Details

Go back to the questions in Exercise 1. While you watch the video, answer the questions.

What About You?

Discuss these questions in a group.

1. How many brothers and sisters do you have?

2. In your culture, is your family considered small, average size or large?

3. What are some chores that were done in your house when you were growing up (washing dishes, sweeping the floor, making beds, etc.)?

4. Who usually did each chore?

5. Did people complain when they had to do chores?

6. Do you do the same chores in Canada? Do you do any new chores, such as shovelling snow?

Families of the World: Mexico

Video Activity 3: Part 2

Exercise 1: Get Ready to Watch the Video

☐ ☐   Read these questions aloud with a partner.

1. Why does Alejandra get to be the referee?

2. Who does Alejandra telephone?

3. Alejandra didn't study karate because she was a girl.   **T   F**

4. The temperature changes often in Puebla.   **T   F**

5. When is the rainy season?

6. What activity is good to do on a rainy day?

7. What are they celebrating?

8. When does the Prado family go to church?

9. How many churches are there in the area around Puebla?

10. Hernan Cortes brought the Catholic religion to Mexico in the sixteenth century.   **T   F**

11. What special event sometimes takes place on Sundays?

12. What is the "cinco de mayo"?

13. When was Benito Juarez president of Mexico?

14. What are enchiladas?

15. What is Aunt Rita's job?

16. Why does Alejandra hate to see the weekend end?

17. A serenade is:

    a) music   b) a dance   c) a food

18. What does the family do together on the weekend?

Exercise 2: Watch the Video for General Ideas

Watch the video. What are some topics that are discussed?

Exercise 3: Watch the Video for Details

Go back to the questions in Exercise 1. While you watch the video, answer the questions.

Family Dinners

Interview another student. Find out about eating customs in other cultures. Use these questions to help you.

1. At what times to you eat meals in your culture?
2. When do you eat your main meal of the day?
3. What are some typical foods you eat for each meal?
4. Which meals do you usually eat with your family?
5. Who usually cooks the food in your family?
6. Who shops for the food in your family?
7. How often do you invite people to your house for a meal?
8. When you left home did you change any of your habits?

My Customs

Write about a traditional get-together in your family. It can be a holiday celebration, a birthday party, an anniversary or any other time your family meets. Write about who is there, what you eat, special clothes you wear, special things you do, etc.

Supplementary Grammar

Reflexive Pronouns

Use the singular ending **self** and the plural ending **selves**.

myself	ourselves
yourself	yourselves
himself herself it itself	themselves

Reflexive pronouns are used as follows:

A. The reflexive pronoun refers to the subject of the sentence.
Example: The student taught **himself** English.

B. The reflexive pronoun with **by** can be substituted for the word **alone**.
Example: I can do this work **alone**.
I can do this work **by myself**.

Exercise 1

Write the correct reflexive pronoun.

1. Annabel and Lisa
2. the principal
3. you and Tanya
4. I
5. the dog
6. Ray and I
7. Andrew and his friends
8. Charles
9. you
10. the teacher

Exercise 2

Complete the following sentences. Use reflexive pronouns.

1. I was alone at the party so I introduced _____.
2. Did you teach _____ to speak English?
3. The students introduced _____.
4. Mark excused _____ and left the room.
5. Amy and I protected _____ from the rain with an umbrella.

6. Richard pushed _____ to finish his work quickly.

7. A cat washes _____ with its tongue.

8. You and Madelyn can cook dinner _____.

9. Charles usually makes _____ lunch.

10. Those people can help _____ to coffee.

Exercise 3

Complete the sentences. Use **by** and a reflexive pronoun to replace the word **alone**.

Example: You can practise pronunciation **by yourself**.

1. You can't practise conversation _____.

2. The girl found the classroom _____.

3. The students planned the party _____.

4. Our hostess cooked the whole dinner _____.

5. Don't try to carry all the books _____.

6. The students chose partners _____.

7. Elevator doors open _____.

8. The subway stopped at the station _____.

9. Thank you, but I can open the door _____.

10. She can find the office _____.

Simple Past Tense

Question Form

Use the auxiliary verb **did** to show simple past time. Use the base form for the main verb.

Example: We ate dinner late.   **Did** you **eat** dinner at 7 o'clock?

Exercise 1

Find the sentences that are correct. Correct the errors in the sentences that are wrong.

1. Did the Bay **had** a sale last week?

2. Did the sales clerk **remember** to charge tax?

3. Did the customer **went to** the fitting room to try on the suit?

4. Did the green dress **fit** the lady very well?

5. Did people always **wore** bathing suits for swimming?
6. Did the customer **decided** to buy the wool jacket?
7. Did you **liked** the new spring styles?
8. Did you **buy** those shoes on sale?
9. Did the customer **paid** by credit card?
10. Did the woman **carry** all the packages by herself?

Exercise 2

These are the answers. Write the questions.

Example: I bought a sweater.   **Did you buy a sweater?**

1. The store put everything on sale.
2. The customers bought things they liked.
3. The tourists wanted to shop while they were here.
4. She went to the fitting room to try on the clothes.
5. She found a mirror in the fitting room.
6. Men wore bathing trunks with tops.
7. The customer asked the price of the rain coat.
8. Everyone paid the GST on their purchases.

Exercise 3

Write seven questions to ask a classmate about his or her activities last weekend. Write yes/no questions in the simple past tense.

Example: **Did you wake up early on Sunday?**

Information Questions

These are the question words:

when

where

what

why

who

how

Exercise 1

Use these words to make questions that match the answers.

Example: at Eaton's   **Where did you buy your dress?**

1. a bathing suit
2. by taxi
3. this morning
4. the shoe department
5. the sales clerk
6. to wear to a party
7. in the fitting room
8. at Sears
9. new shoes
10. It was on sale.

Exercise 2

Write seven questions to ask another student about a new jacket that he or she bought.

Negative Form

Use the auxiliary verb **did** to show simple past time. Add **not** after the auxiliary. Use the base form for the main verb.

Example: We went shopping.   **We did not go skating.**

Exercise 1

Find the sentences that are correct. Correct the errors in the sentences that are wrong.

1. The sales clerk **did not helped** the customer before me.
2. The customer **did not buy** the pair of shoes.
3. People **did not wore** bikinis in the 1920s.
4. The escalator in the department store **did not work** well.
5. Tara **did not thought** the colour was nice.
6. The men's wear department **did not carry** running shoes.
7. The cashier **did not accepted** credit cards.
8. People **did not want** to wait in line at the cash register.

Exercise 2

Make these sentences negative.

Example: The lady took a long time to buy a dress.
The lady did not take a long time to buy a dress.

1. The lady took a long time to choose a skirt.
2. Some people liked the new spring fashions.
3. Clothing in the men's wear department seemed expensive.
4. The tourists went to every store in town.
5. The sales clerk mentioned that there was going to be a sale next week.
6. People bought things with bright colours.
7. That man wore a business suit on Saturday.
8. The new styles shocked the young people.

Note: The contraction of **did not** is **didn't**.

"Some"/"Any"

Use **some** when the sentence is an affirmative statement.

Example: I want to buy **some** red shoes.

Use **any** in negative sentences and in questions.

Example: Do you have **any** red shoes?
No, I don't have **any** red shoes.

Exercise 1

Complete the sentences with **some** or **any**.

1. The customer didn't have _____ time to waste.
2. The sales clerk brought _____ other sizes to the fitting room.
3. Does this store have _____ winter coats for sale?
4. Did you buy _____ shoes there?
5. People wore _____ strange styles in the past.
6. Early this century men didn't wear _____ clothes to go swimming.
7. There are _____ nice wool suits on sale at the Bay.
8. I need to go shopping because I don't have _____ clothes for the party.
9. The customer asked the sales clerk to show her _____ clothes.
10. Is there _____ tax on children's clothing?

Exercise 2

The same rule as for **some/any** is used for **somebody/anybody** and for **something/anything**.

Use the correct word to complete the sentences.

1. I feel shy at this party because I don't know _____.
2. Have you had _____ news from your family?
3. There is _____ strange about that couple.
4. I'm hungry because I didn't have _____ time to eat before the party.
5. The hostess is talking to _____ in the kitchen.
6. There is _____ good food on the table.
7. Giovanni wants to say _____.
8. Ali doesn't want _____ to eat.
9. Can _____ tell me the time?
10. _____ ate all the potato chips.

Adverbs

Adverbs describe verbs. Add **ly** to the adjective form.

Examples: slow   **slowly**

careful   **carefully**

Spelling Rule:

For adjectives that end with **le**, drop the **e** and add **y**

Example: probable   **probably**

For adjectives that end with **y**, change to **i** and add **ly**

Example: easy   **easily**

Exercise 1

Give the adverb form of these adjectives.

1. beautiful
2. quick
3. loud
4. slow
5. careful
6. nice

7. high
8. usual
9. easy
10. serious
11. quick
12. wide

Exercise 2

Complete the sentences with an adjective or an adverb.

1. The hot-air balloon came down _____. (slow)
2. Tourists who go up in the balloon can see the animals _____. (easy)
3. The wind was too _____ for going up in a balloon. (strong)
4. Some balloons were _____ painted. (beautiful)
5. Today ballooning is a _____ activity. (simple)
6. The Montgolfier brothers took their work _____. (serious)
7. The first hot-air balloons were _____. (unusual)
8. Balloonists don't like to go down too _____. (quick)
9. The first dirigibles were steered _____. (careful)
10. People _____ got the idea of flying from the birds. (probable)

Some adverbs do not use the ending **ly**.

fast	fast
hard	hard
low	low
late	late
good	well

Continuous Aspect

The ending **ing** is a signal of continuous action. It does not tell us the tense or time the action took place. Use the auxiliary verb **be** to show the tense.

Present tense	Past tense	Future tense
am	was	will be
is	was	will be
are	were	will be

Example: They **were** asking questions in class yesterday.

They **are** thinking about it now.

They **will** be asking questions tomorrow.

Exercise 1

Find the signals of time in the following sentences. Then decide if the auxiliary verb form of **to be** is correct. Correct sentences if they are wrong.

1. We were watching news clips in class yesterday.
2. Tomorrow in class we were hearing a presentation on Taiwan.
3. I was finishing my exam this morning when the bell rang.
4. I remember the first day of class. Nobody is talking very much.
5. The director is smiling at everyone today.
6. I hated that outing last weekend. My classmates are speaking in Spanish.
7. This morning we ran because the bus was coming.
8. The rain was falling when the plane landed yesterday.
9. Are you eating right now?
10. Before you came over last night I am feeling lonely.

Exercise 2

Write the correct form of the auxiliary verb **to be**.

1. The people at the bus stop _____ standing in line patiently at the moment.
2. The doors of the supermarket _____ closing when I arrived.
3. I can't come now. I _____ writing a letter home.
4. When I entered the lounge, I noticed that some students _____ speaking in Japanese.
5. Next month I _____ going home to visit my family.
6. The listening tape is very hard, so the students _____ not writing.
7. I usually feel nervous when the airplane _____ taking off.
8. We didn't understand the teacher because he _____ speaking too quickly.
9. What _____ happening in this room when I walked in?
10. Don't call after 11 o'clock. I _____ sleeping.

Negative Form

The auxiliary verb and the word **not** are used to make sentences negative.

Example: He was listening.   He **was not** listening.

Exercise 1

Make negative sentences from the words that are given. Use past time.

Example: The students were not talking.

1. talking / the students
2. working / the tape recorder
3. explaining / the teacher
4. studying / Alexander
5. improving / their accents
6. taking / the bus
7. helping / the grammar exercises
8. shouting / the other class

Exercise 2

Write the tense (time) for each sentence. Then change negative sentences to affirmative sentences and affirmative sentences to negative ones.

1. The listening exercises will not be getting easier in the future.
2. The students were not listening to the teacher.
3. Nadia is laughing at her partner.
4. Gaston was sleeping in class this morning.
5. We will not be having an exam next week.
6. The lazy students are not learning very much.
7. We were not having fun during the break.
8. I am planning to go home at the end of the course.

Possessive Pronouns

mine	ours
yours	yours
his hers	theirs

We use possessive pronouns to replace unnecessary nouns.

Example: That car is my car.   That car is **mine**.

Exercise 1

Replace unnecessary nouns with possessive pronouns.

1. Two different people thought the fork on the left was their fork.
2. That salad bowl is my salad bowl.
3. Tanya sat on the chair she thought was her chair.
4. This is my glass. That glass is your glass.
5. The address that we gave to the pizza place was our address.
6. Mr. Clark thought that the last piece of pizza was his piece of pizza.
7. All the places at this table are your places.
8. The recipe for that cake is my recipe.
9. The flowers on the table are your flowers.
10. Nobody knows which plate is his or her plate.

Exercise 2

Write the words that the pronouns replace.

Example: This book is ours.   **our book**

1. The choice of pizza toppings is yours.
2. The Italians say that the original recipe is theirs.
3. Nadia wants pepperoni on her pizza but her sister wants anchovies on hers.
4. The pizza with no anchovies is ours.
5. The address we gave the pizza place is mine.
6. John said that the biggest piece of pizza was his.
7. Italian pizza is tastier than ours.
8. I can't believe that the only pizza with cheese is his.

Exercise 3

Choose the correct answer.

1. Jessica invited _____ (her, hers) friends to dinner.
2. This is _____ (my, mine) spoon. The other one is _____ (you, yours).
3. Excuse me. I think this napkin is _____ (my, mine).
4. The cake we are eating isn't _____ (our, ours).
5. Elizabeth's friends said that the salad was _____ (their, theirs).
6. _____ (My, mine) piece of cake is smaller than _____ (her, hers).
7. The salad she is serving is _____ (their, theirs).
8. Pass the butter that is near _____ (your, yours) plate.

"Should"

Should can be used to give advice.

Example: You are tired.   You **should** relax for a while.

Should can also be used for stronger suggestions.

Example: The sidewalk is slippery. You **should** be careful.

Exercise 1

Respond to these statements by offering advice with **should**.

Example: I'm too fat.   You **should** eat less.

1. You like to cook.
2. John feels hungry.
3. This meat has no taste.
4. This restaurant looks too expensive.
5. This waiter is giving us really good service.
6. I don't like cola.
7. My hamburger is very small.
8. There is a mistake in the bill.
9. My girlfriend doesn't like fast food.
10. This table is too small for three people.

Exercise 2

Some things are not advisable. Respond to these statements by offering advice with **should not**. The contraction of **should not** is **shouldn't**.

Example: I'm full.   You **shouldn't** eat any more.

1. I can't sleep if I drink coffee.
2. This coffee is too strong.
3. No one in our group really likes hamburgers.
4. Janet left her purse on the table.
5. It is expensive to eat in a restaurant every lunch hour.
6. He loves dessert but he is getting fat.
7. My friend went shopping at lunch time and now she is hungry.
8. I know sweets are bad for me.

Count and Non-count

How many asks a question about things that you can count:

    friends

    hours

    sports

    cups of tea

    animals

How much asks a question about things that you can't count:

    money

    rain

    time

    coffee

    sugar

Exercise 1

Questions use **how much** and **how many** to ask about quantity.

Read the questions. Change the questions that are incorrect.

1. How much money should I bring with me?
2. How many dollars should I exchange at the bank?
3. How much tourists came here last year?
4. How much sports can you play at the hotel?
5. How much does a hotel room cost?
6. How many times did you telephone the airline?
7. How much is a peso worth in Canadian money?
8. How much rooms does that hotel have?
9. How many hours did you wait at the airport?
10. How much people took the flight?
11. How many weeks holiday do you have?
12. How many time did you spend in Hawaii?

Exercise 2

Much and **many** are used in negative statements.

Examples: He doesn't have **much** money with him.

He didn't send **many** postcards to his family and friends.

Make negative sentences with **much** or **many**.

Example: My friend didn't get **much** sleep last night.

1. time
2. snow
3. activities
4. rooms
5. help
6. hours

Exercise 3

Affirmative statements use **a lot of** with count and non-count words.

Example: How much snow is there in Canada?

Affirmative: There **is a lot of** snow in most places.

Negative: There **isn't much** snow in Vancouver.

Answer the following questions using **a lot of** if the answer is affirmative and **much** or **many** if it is negative.

Example: How **much** sun do you have in your country?

We have **a lot of** sun.

1. How many people live in China?
2. How many people live in Vancouver?
3. How much pollution is there in Mexico City?
4. How many people live in the capital of your country?
5. How many people like opera?
6. How much does popcorn cost?
7. How much does a taxi cost in Paris?
8. How many hours does it take to cross the Pacific ocean?
9. How much rain falls in your country in a year?
10. How many people in the world speak Swedish?

Simple Past/Past Continuous

Actions in past time can be simple.

Example: I **talked** a lot yesterday.

Actions in past time can be continuous.

Example: He **was talking** all morning.

Exercise 1

Use the past tense. Choose the simple or continuous form of the verb.

1. The students in the last class usually _____ on time. (arrive)
2. When I looked into the classroom, the teacher _____. (talk).
3. Annabel _____ much faster than Lisa. (speak).
4. Simon was absent. Maybe he _____. (sleep)
5. The class _____ when I arrived. (start)
6. That teacher usually _____ the lessons interesting. (make)
7. Last term those two boys _____ to class late nearly every day. (come)
8. We listened carefully when the Brazilian student _____ her presentation. (give)
9. Many students _____ nervous the first day in class. (feel)
10. I didn't hear the instructions because I _____ my pencil. (look for)

Exercise 2

If an action takes place in past time and you use two clauses in the sentence to describe the action, follow these rules:

Use the simple past tense with a **when** clause.

Example: The ice melted **when spring came**.

Use the past continuous with a **while** clause.

Example: It rained **while we were walking home**.

Read the sentences. Change the verb if it is not correct.

1. While I was sitting in the garden, I noticed the clouds.
2. The cows were happy when the farmer opened the gate.
3. He was ploughing the field while I rested.
4. When he planted seeds, he was careful.
5. The farmer got out the tractor when he was seeing the snow melt.

6. The birds sang while the sun shone.
7. The birds looked for corn in the fields when they were arriving.
8. When the snow melted, I knew that spring was coming.
9. The weather was warmer when winter was ending.
10. The rain started while we were ploughing the field.

Exercise 3

Complete the sentences.

1. The tractor stopped working while _____.
2. The cows left the barn when _____.
3. When _____, we knew it was spring.
4. While _____, I sat on the fence and watched.
5. We stayed in the barn while _____.
6. The trees began to turn green when _____.
7. The farmer planted the seeds when _____.
8. They prepared the seeds while _____.
9. We knew winter was over when _____.
10. While _____, the rain stopped.

"Will"

Use **will** as an auxiliary verb to express future time.
Example: Snow **will** fall in winter.

Use **will not** to express negation in future time.
The contraction of **will not** is **won't**.
Example: Snow **won't** fall in summer.

Exercise 1

Write sentences about the Arctic in winter. Use **will** to say what will happen to:

1. the temperature
2. the birds
3. some animals
4. the weather
5. the Arctic Ocean
6. the days
7. the Inuit

Exercise 2

Think about these statements. If they are not accurate, change the auxiliary verb.

Example: It **will** snow in Indonesia this year.   It **will not** snow in Indonesia.

1. Birds will fly south in the spring.
2. The Inuit will use sleds to travel on the snow.
3. A lot of snow will fall in the Arctic this year.
4. The days will get longer and longer in winter.
5. The Inuit won't keep their customs.
6. Polar bears will hunt seals on the sea ice.
7. The Inuit won't make many things from the walrus.
8. The days will get shorter in winter.
9. Temperatures will drop in the winter.
10. Flowers will come out in the fall.
11. Migration will take place in winter and summer.
12. The Arctic Ocean will freeze in winter.

Exercise 3

Write seven sentences about things that will happen when the seasons change in your country.

Comparative Adjectives

To form comparisons with adjectives that have one syllable, add **er**.
Example: tall   **taller**

To form comparisons with longer adjectives, use **more**.
Example: popular   **more popular**

Exercise 1

Find the adjective in each sentence. Then write the comparative form.
Example: Hockey is a fast game.   (**faster**)

1. Downhill skiing can be a dangerous sport.
2. Tennis builds strong muscles.
3. Lacrosse is an old sport.
4. Figure-skating is beautiful to watch.

5. Roller-skating had an interesting beginning.
6. Weight lifting is a hard sport to practise.
7. Aerobics is a new activity at the YWCA.
8. Judo is a difficult sport to learn.
9. Swimming is not a very expensive sport.
10. Ski-jumping is exciting to watch.

Exercise 2

When you write a sentence that compares two things, use the comparative form of the adjective and **than**.

Examples: Moscow is **colder than** Paris.

Paris is **more beautiful than** New York.

Note that comparisons can be made with **more** or **less**. Look at the examples.

Caviar is more expensive than rice.

The bus is less expensive than the plane.

Use this list of adjectives. Write sentences that compare different cities in the world.

Example: (crowded) Hong Kong is **more** crowded than Vancouver.

(big) Mexico City is **bigger** than Rome.

1. dangerous   4. hot   7. expensive   10. popular
2. small   5. polluted   8. modern
3. humid   6. busy   9. clean

Superlative Adjectives

To form superlatives with adjectives that have one syllable, add **the** before the adjective and **est** after it.

Example: a kind person   **the kindest** person

To form superlatives with adjectives that have more than one syllable, use **the most** before the adjective.

Example: a common name   **the most** common name

Exercise 1

Find the adjective in the sentence. Then write the superlative form.

Example: Fencing is a difficult sport.   **the most difficult sport**

1. Polo is a dangerous sport.
2. Hockey players are fast skaters.
3. Sumo wrestling is an unusual sport.

4. Cricket is a slow game.

5. Football is an old sport.

6. Roller-skating has a strange history.

7. Sumo wrestlers are very strong.

8. Downhill skiing is an exciting sport.

9. Some sports are really violent.

10. Soccer is a wonderful sport.

Exercise 2

Use superlatives to make sentences.

Example: Swimming is **the best** exercise.

1. good

2. exciting

3. popular

4. fast

5. hard

6. cold

7. tiring

8. boring

9. nice

10. difficult

"Can"/"Could"

Use **could** to form the past tense of **can**.

Example: We **can** save electricity by turning off the lights.

In the past, people **could** live without electricity.

Exercise 1

Complete these sentences with **can** or **could**.

1. Twenty-five years ago people _____ swim in most lakes in Canada.

2. Today people _____ not swim in many lakes and rivers.

3. In the past farmers _____ find rich land easily.

4. Animals _____ live safely in the Amazon rainforest before people began cutting trees.

5. We _____ recycle glass jars but not plastic ones.

6. Many offices have boxes where employees _____ recycle paper.

7. Ecologists don't know if they _____ stop pollution.

8. For a long time people _____ see that pollution was dangerous.

Exercise 2

Write six sentences about things you can't do today but you could do in the past.

Example: In my country I **could** go to the beach every day.

"Have to"

Use **have** to to express necessity or mild obligation.

Example: I **have to** meet my friend after class.

Exercise 1

Complete these sentences. Say what you have to do when:

Example: You feel tired. **You have to sleep.**

1. the bus is full
2. you forget your bus pass
3. the subway reaches the last station
4. all the seats on the bus are taken
5. your car is out of gas
6. you are late for work
7. you want to change buses
8. you don't have a student card
9. you see a No Smoking sign
10. you don't know which subway to take

Exercise 2

Make a list of seven things you have to do this week.

Example: I **have to** get my hair cut.

Geographical Directions

Nouns that describe geographical directions have adjective forms.

east	eastern
west	western
north	northern
south	southern

Exercise 1

Combine these sentences.

Example: The Arctic is in Canada.

It is in the north.

The Arctic is in northern Canada.

1. The Inuit live in Canada. They live in the north.
2. Alaska is in North America. It is in the northwest.
3. Chao Jie comes from a different culture. It is in the east.
4. England is an example of a culture. It is in the west.
5. Florida is a state. It is in the south.
6. Anne has an accent. It is from the south.
7. Canada and Norway are countries. They are in the north.
8. Gabrielle likes to look at the sky. She looks to the south.
9. Newfoundland is a province. It is in the east.
10. Vancouver and Toronto are two cities. Vancouver is to the west. Toronto is to the east.

Exercise 2

Use direction words to complete these sentences.

1. Marseille is a city in _____ France.
2. Vancouver is in the _____ of Canada.
3. Singapore is _____ of the equator.
4. Hong Kong is an _____ city.
5. Japan is in the _____ Pacific.
6. Australia is _____ of the equator.
7. Colombia is in _____ South America.
8. Finland is in _____ Europe.
9. Brazil is _____ of Chile.
10. New York is in the _____ United States.

Common Irregular Verbs

Present	Past	Present	Past	Present	Past
bear	bore	go	went	sell	sold
begin	began	grow	grew	send	sent
bite	bit	have	had	shine	shone
bleed	bled	hear	heard	shoot	shot
blow	blew	hide	hid	show	showed
break	broke	hit	hit	shrink	shrank
bring	brought	hold	held	shut	shut
build	built	keep	kept	sing	sang
buy	bought	know	knew	sink	sank
can	could*	lead	led	sit	sat
catch	caught	leave	left	sleep	slept
choose	chose	lend	lent	speak	spoke
come	came	let	let	spend	spent
cost	cost	lie	lay	spin	spun
cut	cut	lose	lost	spread	spread
do	did	make	made	stand	stood
draw	drew	may	might*	steal	stole
drink	drank	mean	meant	swim	swam
drive	drove	meet	met	take	took
eat	ate	pay	paid	teach	taught
fall	fell	put	put	tear	tore
fight	fought	quit	quit	tell	told
find	found	read	read†	think	thought
fly	flew	ride	rode	throw	threw
forget	forgot	ring	rang	try	tried
forgive	forgave	rise	rose	understand	understood
freeze	froze	run	ran	wake	woke
fry	fried	say	said	wear	wore
get	got	see	saw	win	won
give	gave	shake	shook	write	wrote

* One use of the auxiliaries **could** and **might** is as the past tense of the verbs **can** and **may**.

† Note that the pronunciation changes in the past tense to "red."

Community
Contact Tasks

In the Community

Task #1

The Party Clothes Task

Work with a partner. Go to a department store or a clothing store. Put together an exciting outfit that you would like to wear to a fancy party. Pretend that money is no object.

1.   On the worksheet, check the items that your outfit includes.

hat	tie	dress
hair accessories	scarf	suit
jewellery	belt	vest
jacket	pants	high-heeled shoes
blouse	skirt	flat shoes
shirt	stockings	shoes with laces
sweater	socks	loafers

2.   List the things that you checked. Then put them in the chart on the worksheet.

Item	Colour	Price	Description

3.   Draw and label your outfit.

In the Community

Task #2

The Fruit Task

Work with a partner. Go to a fruit store. Try to get the following information:

	Type	Colour	Price	Where it comes from
apples				
oranges				
grapes				

Name three other fruits.

1. Draw and label each kind of fruit.

2. Where does it come from?

3. How much does it cost?

In the Community

Task #3

The Crunchy Munchy Task

Look at the labels on foods you have in your house. You can also look in the supermarket and at food ads in the newspaper or in magazines. Find as many foods as you can that belong in each category.

creamy	
crunchy	
crisp	**potato chips**
juicy	
salty	**peanuts**
smooth	
spicy	
bubbly	

In the Community

Task #4

The Dairy Task

Work with a partner. Go to a supermarket. Find the dairy section. Look for information to complete the charts. Use the worksheet.

	Types	Brands	Type of package	Prices
milk	skim, etc.			
cheese				$2.75
sour cream			plastic container	

	Flavours	Brands	Sizes or quantities	Prices
ice cream				
yoghurt				

List two other products you can find in the dairy section. Give the quantity and price of each.

	Product	Quantity	Price
1.			
2.			

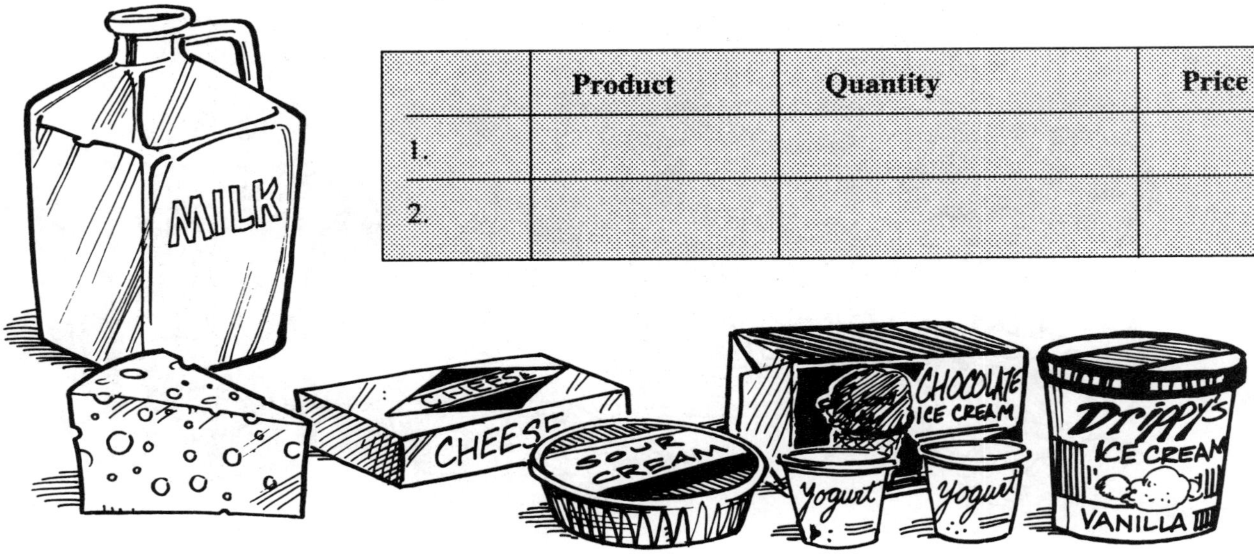

In the Community

Task #5

The Junk Food Task

1. Name five places you can buy junk food.
2. Work with a partner. Go to one of the places. Fill in the chart. Use the worksheet.

	Kinds	Sizes	Prices
gum			
chocolate bar			
potato chips			
corn chips			
hard candy			
licorice			
popcorn			
ice cream snacks			
other			

3. Choose three products. Eat them and describe them.

In the Community

Task #6

The Fast Food, Junk Mail Task

Collect four flyers for food that you can order in. (If you live in a house, they come in your mail slot. If you live in an apartment, they are often left in the lobby.)

Name of restaurant	Kind of food	Items available	Cost

1. Write the information in the chart on the worksheet.

2. Is there a charge for delivery?

3. Compare your chart with a partner's chart.

   a) What foods do you have that are the same?

   b) Are the prices the same?

   c) What foods do you have that are different?

4. Did you ever order food this way? Describe the experience.

In the Community

Task #7

The Bank Task

1. Go to your bank, or a bank near you. Find out the following:

    a) How many kinds of accounts does the bank have?

    b) Fill in the chart on the worksheet. Check (✔) the services available for each account.

	Earn interest	Write a cheque	Have a bank book	Pay service charges
chequing account				
savings account				
combination account				
daily interest account				
other				

2. Who can get a bank card?

3. What information does the application form ask for?

4. What services can you get with a bank card?

In the Community

Task #8

The Y

A. Look in the white pages of the phone book. Write the address of the Y that is closest to you.

B. Find the best route to the Y by bus or subway. With a partner, visit the Y.

1. What fitness activities does the Y have?

    a) swimming   e) badminton

    b) aerobics   f) volleyball

    c) weight lifting   g) basketball

    d) self-defence courses   h) raquetball

2. Name an activity that is not a sport.

3. Name an activity that is interesting to you.

4. Find out the rules for participating in the activity that you are interested in.

5. How much is a yearly membership?

    a) for an adult   d) for a senior

    b) for a child   e) for a family

    c) for a student

In the Community

Task # 9

The Recycling Task

1. Go to a grocery store. Look for the following items. On the worksheet, check (✔) the containers that these foods come in.

Soup	Cookies	Fruit Juice	Cheese
box	box	can	wooden box
can	paper bag	jar	plastic container
jar	cellopahane wrapped	carton	wrapped in plastic
envelope		plastic bottle	wrapped in paper
plastic container (if frozen)		cardboard container (if frozen)	on a styrofoam tray
		drinking box	foil wrapped

2. List all the containers that are easy to recycle.

3. List all the containers that are difficult to recycle.

4. How can you carry these items home from the store you visit?
   a) in a plastic bag
   b) in a paper bag
   c) in a cloth bag

5. Did you bring your own bag?